T0329221

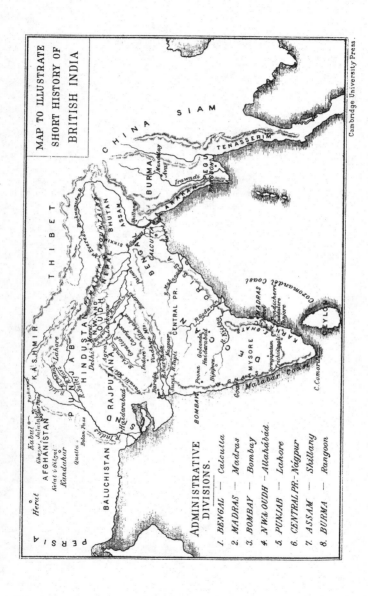

MAP TO ILLUSTRATE
SHORT HISTORY OF
BRITISH INDIA

Cambridge University Press.

ADMINISTRATIVE
DIVISIONS.

1. BENGAL — Calcutta
2. MADRAS — Madras
3. BOMBAY — Bombay
4. NW & OUDH — Allahábád.
5. PUNJAB — Lahore
6. CENTRAL PR.-Nágpur
7. ASSAM — Shillong
8. BURMA — Rangoon

# A SHORT HISTORY

### OF

# BRITISH INDIA.

## E. S. CARLOS, M.A.,

### TRINITY COLLEGE, CAMBRIDGE;
### LATE HEAD MASTER OF EXETER GRAMMAR SCHOOL.

### AT THE UNIVERSITY PRESS.

London: C. J. CLAY AND SONS,
### CAMBRIDGE UNIVERSITY PRESS WAREHOUSE,
### AVE MARIA LANE.
### 1889

CAMBRIDGE UNIVERSITY PRESS
Cambridge, New York, Melbourne, Madrid, Cape Town,
Singapore, São Paulo, Delhi, Mexico City

Cambridge University Press
The Edinburgh Building, Cambridge CB2 8RU, UK

Published in the United States of America by Cambridge University Press, New York

www.cambridge.org
Information on this title: www.cambridge.org/9781107621831

First published 1889
First paperback edition 2013

A catalogue record for this publication is available from the British Library

ISBN 978-1-107-62183-1 Paperback

# PREFACE.

THIS *Short History of British India* is intended to give a complete outline of the circumstances which have produced the present political and social condition of India. The details are to be found in the books on which it is based.

Such an account of India may prove of service as a School-book by supplying information, which seems a proper part of every boy's education in these days, when so many are taught to look forward to an honourable career in some of the various Civil and Military Services of India, or in the new field of Indian Plantations.

I am indebted to 'old Indian' friends for the correction of those chapters which relate to the physical geography of the country and the condition of native life under British rule.

E. S. C.

# NOTE.

Indian names are spelt according to the *Imperial Gazetteer of India* edited by Sir W. W. Hunter, which represents the system adopted in India by the authority of the Indian Government in 1870. It is based on the system of Sir W. Jones, which was popularised in Elphinstone's History of India, 1841. A few names which have acquired popular currency are left unaltered.

---

The vowel sounds are represented and sounded thus :

| a | á | e | i | í |
|---|---|---|---|---|
| rur*a*l | f*a*r | gr*ey* | f*i*ll | d*ee*r |

| o | u | ú | ai |
|---|---|---|---|
| b*o*ne | b*u*ll | r*u*de | l*y*re |

The consonants are to be sounded as in English, except *g, ch, s, t,* which are only sounded as the corresponding letters in *give, church, solstice, tin.*

# AUTHORITIES USED.

### 1. HINDU RELIGION AND PHILOLOGY.

MAX MÜLLER.   Chips from a German Workshop.
,,               Lectures on the Science of Language.
,,               Sacred Books of the East : vol. xi. *Buddhist Suttas*, translated from Pâli, by T. W. Rhys Davids ; vol. xix. *Life of Buddha*, translated from Chinese, by S. Beal.
MONIER WILLIAMS.   Hinduism.   RHYS DAVIDS.   Buddhism.
LYALL.   Asiatic Studies.

### 2. MOHAMMEDAN PERIOD.

GIBBON.   Decline and Fall of Roman Empire.
ELPHINSTONE.   History of India.
TALBOYS WHEELER.   History of India (Hindu and Mohammedan).

### 3. ENGLISH PERIOD.

ORME.   Indostan (1745—1761).
MILL.   History of British India, continued by WILSON.
KAYE.   War in Afghanistan (1839—42).
,,         History of Sepoy War.
SEELEY.   Expansion of England.
NAPIER.   Life of General Sir Charles Napier.
BOSWORTH SMITH.   Life of Sir John Lawrence.
MAHON'S History of England, ALISON'S History of Europe, BRIGHT'S History of England.
Annual Register and various Reviews.

### 4. PHYSICAL GEOGRAPHY, STATISTICS, AND GENERAL INFORMATION.

The Imperial Gazetteer, edited by Sir W. W. HUNTER for the Indian Government, 1870.
HEBER (Bishop of Calcutta).   Narrative of a Journey (1824—5).
MONEIR WILLIAMS.   Modern India, 1878.
STRACHEY.   India, 1888.

# CONTENTS.

# A SHORT HISTORY OF BRITISH INDIA.

## CHAPTER I. INDIA. PHYSICAL FEATURES.

**Extent of India.** The Indian Empire extends at present over the territories of India and Burma, with a certain political influence over the countries of Afghánistán and Baluchistán, and thus includes or affects a large part of the southern districts of Asia.

**Name of India.** India is the name now used by English people to describe the country which stretches southward from the Himálayas as a great promontory into the Indian Ocean. For a long time it was called the **East Indies** to distinguish it from the West Indies, or West India Islands, which when first discovered by Columbus were supposed to belong to the continent of Asia, then usually called by the vague name—India. The use of this name is due to the historians of the conquests of Alexander the Great, who penetrated into the Punjab and descended the Indus to the sea. They described the people as **Indi** from the Persian form of **Sind,** the native name of that district. From the Persians also came the name **Hindustan,** meaning the country of the Hindus, which is employed by them to describe the plains of the Indus and the Ganges,

C.

but has been used by English writers for the whole country. There is properly no native name for the country as a whole.

**Name—Burma.** The name—**Burma**—represents closely the pronunciation of the name by which the natives of that country call themselves. Burma is sometimes called **Further India.**—There is no real connexion of race, language, religion or geography, between Burma and India, properly so called, but the term is convenient as it allows the name **India** to be used for the whole Indian Empire.

**Physical Geography.** Some knowledge of the physical geography of the countries which are included in the Indian Empire is necessary as an introduction to their history. The size of India is realised most distinctly by a knowledge of its great mountain-ranges, plains, and rivers. Its political divisions are easily understood from its geographical features. The peculiarities of its boundaries have clearly defined the direction of immigration and invasion. The fertility of the country, natural and artificial, has supplied the inducement for conquest and settlement. The actual productions of the land have determined the nature of the trade, the employments, and, to some extent, the character of the people.

**Boundaries of India.** India stretches into the Indian Ocean as a mighty promontory, whose coast-lines start from the mouths of the Indus and the Ganges, and run roughly south-east and south-west, terminating in Cape Comorin. The island of Ceylon is somewhat east of the apex, and judging from the shallowness of the sea which separates it from the mainland, and from its geological structure, it must be considered to belong to the Indian continent, but politically it is a Crown colony, and not subordinate to the Indian Government.

The boundaries of India on the north are determined by ranges of mighty mountains, in which are the sources of the various rivers that form the river-systems of the Indus and the Ganges. These are the mountain ranges of Baluchistán and Afghánistán on the west, and the Himálayas on the north and east. There are few openings in this mountain barrier, but two are of the greatest historical interest. One, at the north-west corner, where the Kábul river joins the Indus, has been the gateway to India from the west, and the other, where the Brahma-putra breaks through the Himálayas at the eastern end, has been the gateway by which Indian influence has passed to Thibet and China.

**The plains of India.** From the Himálayas to the mountains of central India extends a vast plain, which owes its formation and character to the rivers which flow from the range and form the streams and tributaries of the Indus and the Ganges. The plains of the tributaries of the Indus are known as the **Punjab**, or land of the five rivers; that of the lower Indus as **Sind**; while the country watered by the Ganges and the rivers connected with it, is properly called **Hindustan.**

**Southern India.** The centre of the promontory is a fairly regular triangular table-land. Its east and west sides are ranges of mountains parallel to the coast-lines, and called the Eastern and Western Gháts. Its northern side is formed by the hilly ranges known as the Vindhyá and Sátpura mountains, which are the southern boundary of the plains. The Vindhyá and Sátpura ranges form two parallel valleys, through which flow the Narbadá and the Tápti, the only large rivers of the western side of southern India.

The Western Gháts are close to the coast-line and leave only a narrow strip of country at their base; but the Eastern Gháts are at a considerable distance from the coast, and

the strip of low country between the mountains and the sea
is nearly 100 miles broad.

**Rivers.**  The Eastern Gháts are an ill-defined range of
no great height, but the Western Gháts are the watershed of
the rivers of southern India.  Those on their western side
are violent torrents, but on the eastern side rise noble rivers,
as the Mahánadi, the Godávari, and the Kistna, which
flowing through the high country of the centre, pierce
through the Eastern Gháts, and carry down a burden of
precious silt, to be spread over the plains of the lower
country or added to the deltas at the rivers' mouths.  The
rivers of southern India depend entirely on the rain-fall,
and the volume of their water consequently varies much.
It is immense in the rainy season, but insignificant during
the rest of the year.  The Indus and the Ganges and the
rivers connected with them, and the Brahma-putra, are
further affected by the melting of the snow in the Hima-
layas, and their volume is thus maintained throughout the
year.  In time of flood the rivers overflow their banks, and
deposit a layer of fertilising mud on the fields, enabling the
natives to produce most excellent crops with very rude
husbandry.  This is particularly the case in the lower parts
of their course, and in the deltas at their mouths.

In the higher parts of the rivers the water is applied to
the land by **irrigation canals,** which leave the main
stream at some convenient point, and are carried parallel to
the rivers at a higher level.  In the still higher parts, where
the river would dwindle away in the hot season to a petty
stream, the water is stored up for irrigation purposes in the
so-called **tanks.**  These are great reservoirs, made by con-
structing a bank of earth or a solid dam of masonry across
the mouth of a valley through which the river flows.  Thus
an artificial lake is created, capable in some cases of hold-

ing water enough to last a district for two years. Sometimes smaller rivers are converted into a succession of tanks by dams thrown across them at suitable places, each tank supplying a set of irrigation channels.

**Rain-fall.** There is a certain regularity in the time of the rain-fall of the country, owing to the prevalence of periodic winds, known as the south-west and north-east monsoons. The more important is the south-west monsoon, which blows from June to October and brings the rains on which the cultivation of the country depends. The rainy season usually opens with violent thunderstorms and terrific downpours of rain, but in its general character the rainy season is much like an English wet summer. The amount of the rain-fall however varies considerably, and exposes those parts which rely only on the rain-fall for cultivation to the risks of drought and famine.

**Cultivated India.** In the deltas of the rivers the ordinary crop is **rice**. **Wheat** and **millet** are grown in the higher parts. There are usually two sowings,—one, for millet, which is sown as soon as the ground can be prepared after the beginning of the rains, and reaped in the autumn, and the other for wheat, which is sown just before the cessation of the rains in October, and reaped in the spring. Cotton is cultivated in central India, and indigo in Bengal; opium is only allowed to be grown in certain limited districts of Bengal and central India. In recent times the cultivation of tea in the Himálayas and Ceylon, of coffee in the Western Gháts and of chinchona in the Nílgiri hills of southern India, has been introduced and carried on with great success.

The only part of the country that does not lend itself to cultivation is the eastern part of Sind, where there is a large tract of sandy desert, stretching to the Aravalli hills, which separate the basins of the Indus and the Ganges.

**Wild India.** Splendid forests are found, especially on the Western Gháts, and the slopes of the Himálayas. There is a special department of the Government charged with the preservation and management of them, and they are becoming an important source of revenue.

**Animal life.** The forests are the home of the elephant and tiger and of many other wild animals. Numerous kinds of antelope and deer live in the open country and plunder the crops of the villagers. Monkeys abound in the jungles and wherever there are trees. Snakes, harmless and dangerous, are found everywhere, with innumerable birds, and an exuberance of every form of insect life. The chief domestic animals of India are oxen and buffaloes for agricultural purposes and draught. The horse and the elephant are used for military and state purposes. The camel is largely used for riding and carriage. Sheep of an inferior kind, and goats, which are kept in large numbers, supply flesh meat for Europeans and Mohammedans. The food of the Hindus is almost entirely vegetable, consisting of boiled rice, or grain, dressed with **ghi** (clarified butter) and seasoned with spices. Dogs, jackals, and pigs, vultures and kites, are the scavengers.

**Physical geography of Burma.** The physical features of Burma are like those of the valleys of the great Indian rivers. The Irawadi and its tributaries, rising in the mountains of the north, drain a vast basin. A simple husbandry cultivates the lower ground of the valleys through which they flow, the uplands are clothed with splendid forests, and the mouths of the rivers form a grand delta of the same character as the deltas of the Ganges and the Indus.

## CHAPTER II. The Peoples of India.

THE peoples of India may be divided into two grand classes, the **civilised peoples,** who cultivate the ground and live in villages, towns and cities, and the **uncivilised peoples,** found all through India, living in the forests and jungles, and less accessible parts of the country, and known generally as 'hill tribes.' These live by hunting, and have no towns or villages, but come into communication with the civilised peoples for the purposes of trade, to obtain salt, and other things which they cannot produce, in barter for jungle produce of various kinds.

**Primitive peoples of India.** As the hill tribes inhabit the least desirable and most inaccessible parts of the country they are considered to represent primitive peoples, who were driven from the lower lands by the immigration into the country of the peoples who now inhabit and cultivate the plains. The study of the habits of these hill tribes may therefore give us some idea of the earliest state of India. This would lead us to conclude that in very early times the country was occupied by tribes of black hunterfolk, whose food was the game of the forests and jungles, with millet and rice, cultivated, as at the present day, in rough clearings, made by burning the forest near the places where they settled for a time. They may have made intoxicating drinks from the flowers of the mhowa-tree or the sap of the coco-palm, but they probably had no knowledge of weaving, or of the use of the metals, but employed stone and bone for their weapons and tools.

**The Hindus.** The peoples of the plains according to their own traditions entered India from the north-west in successive immigrations. They gradually spread down the valleys of the Indus and the Ganges, conquered and absorbed some part of the people whom they found occupying the country, and forced the rest, the bolder and more warlike tribes, whom they could not subdue, into the mountainous parts of the central plateau and the slopes of the Himálayas. The invaders, with the peoples whom they absorbed, are represented by the **Hindus** of to-day, but their name for themselves when they entered the country was **Aryan** (noble). The language which they spoke is still preserved, though only as a written language, like Latin. This language, as it is the language in which the sacred literature of the Hindu religion is written, is called **Sanskrit**, meaning the polished or literary language as distinguished from the vernacular languages of India. The intimate connexion between Sanskrit and the chief languages of ancient and modern Europe may be accepted as conclusive proof that the Aryan invaders belonged to the same stock as the Teutonic nations of Europe, and the term Indo-European is used to describe one of the great families into which philologists divide the languages of the world.

The modern languages of northern and central India are simply developments of Sanskrit modified by admixture with the languages of the peoples with whom the Aryans amalgamated. In the south languages belonging to another philological division, known as Turanian, prevail, of which the chief are Tamil and Telugu, the languages of the Coromandel or eastern coast, indicating the presence and preponderance there of the earlier races.

Amalgamation of races has generally been a natural and necessary consequence of intercourse, whether commercial or military, but the complete amalgamation of the Aryan immigrants with the earlier races was hindered by the growth of the peculiar characteristic of Indian life, the restrictions of **caste**.

**Hindu castes.** All Hindus now belong by birth to the class, or caste, of their parents, which determines for their whole life their trade or profession, and position in society. There are four castes recognised in the books of the sacred law of the Hindus, **Bráhmans, Kshatriyas, Vaisyas,** and **Súdras,** representing religion, war, agriculture and service. Two of these four castes are still recognisable. The **Bráhmans** are still the priestly caste, though they now engage in other professions. The **Kshatriyas,** the warrior caste of ancient India, are represented by the Rájputs of to-day. The old divisions of Vaisyas and Súdras are however altogether lost, and are replaced by a multitude of castes, formed out of the commercial and industrial classes, which seem to have originated partly in local jealousy of strangers, and partly in the gradual subdivision of trades. Some castes represent religious sects.

**Origin of caste.** The two castes of Bráhmans and Rájputs, the priestly and the soldier castes, have an acknowledged pre-eminence everywhere, and while Hindus of other castes seem to represent the fusion of the immigrant and the earlier races, those who belong to the Bráhman and Rájput castes may be regarded as of pure Aryan descent. In corroboration of this, it may be noticed that Bráhmans and Rájputs are comparatively fair in colour, whereas the rest of the Hindus are dark. This has suggested that the institution of caste arose from the efforts of the immigrant Aryans to preserve their distinction from the earlier races whom they had subdued. It would thus be analogous to institutions of other branches of the Aryan race. The distinctions between Patricians and Plebeians in early Roman history are supposed to indicate that the Patricians were conquerors and the Plebeians a conquered people, and the relations between Spartans and Helots in Lacedæmon imply similar conditions.

**Caste duties.**    Whatever may have been the origin of caste, its restrictions are now regarded as of religious obligation.    The various castes cannot intermarry, or eat together, and are therefore kept apart by social restrictions as well as by the less artificial distinctions of profession.    There is however something beneficial in the trade castes, which act very much like the medieval trade-guilds, securing the training of their members, regulating their work, supervising their conduct, and providing for their support in old age.

**Peoples of Burma.**    The peoples of Burma consist of several races, known as Burmese, Shans, Chins, Karens, Talaings, all belonging to the Turanian family of nations. These people seem to have entered the country from the north at different periods and gradually made their way down the Irawadi valley.    The Burmese appear to be the latest immigrants, being the dominant race, and occupying the valleys and most desirable parts of the country.    Burma seems to have received its civilisation from India during the time of the predominance of Buddhism in India.    Some of the Burmese traditions seem to point to a Rájput immigration.

## CHAPTER III.    RELIGIONS OF INDIA.

AT the present day there are five religions prevalent more or less widely in the Indian Empire, besides the Christian religion.    These are Hinduism and Buddhism, Mohammedanism, the Parsi, and the Síkh religions.

The origin of Hinduism and Buddhism belongs to the early period of Indian history. They may both be regarded as the outcome of an earlier religion represented by the Vedas.

**Vedic religion.** Of late years European scholars have edited and translated the Vedas and other sacred books of Hinduism, and have concluded from their study of these books that the ancient religion of the Aryans as described in the hymns (mantras) of the most ancient of the Hindu sacred books, the Rig-Veda (Veda of Praise), was a simple nature-worship, in which fire, water, earth, sky, sun and moon, clouds and natural phenomena were regarded as manifestations of the presence of the Deity.

**Hindu religious reformers.** A religion such as this might be expected to degenerate into the mere performance of propitiatory rites and ceremonies by the priestly caste. That such degeneration actually took place seems certain from the fact that the religious teachers who arose from time to time in India, and claimed more or less distinctly the authority of a divine mission, always insisted on the religious obligation of personal duties. These religious teachers were independent of the Bráhmans, though not necessarily antagonistic to them. Sometimes indeed they were actually Bráhmans. They correspond in a way to the founders of the schools of Philosophy amongst the Greeks and Romans, both in their influence on practical conduct, and in their relation to the religious ideas of the people.

**Buddha.** The most famous of these religious teachers is **Gautama Buddha. Buddha** is a title which means a **heaven-sent teacher,** and signified that Gautama claimed to have a divine mission to enlighten men by giving them spiritual knowledge. His date is uncertain, but if the latest date for his death, that of the Thibetan Buddhists, be taken, he lived about the time of Alexander the Great. It must however be acknowledged that Buddha's teaching contains no trace of the influence of Greek Philosophy. The characteristic feature of Buddhist teaching is the inculcation of the three duties, of control over self, kindness to other men, and respect for the life of all creatures.

**Story of Buddha's life and teaching.** From Buddhist accounts it would appear that Gautama was the only son of a Rájput rájá of a principality in the northern part of the country, afterwards called Oudh. In spite of his position he seems to have been profoundly unhappy, and to have felt deeply the sadness of the ordinary lot of human life, especially in the forms of old age, disease, and death. At last he could endure his princely life no longer, and resolved to abandon it for a life of asceticism, in hopes of finding some way of escape from this misery for himself and others. He is described as stopped for the moment by the grief of his father at his determination; but his purpose was unchanged, and at night, attended by his faithful servant, he rode forth from the palace into the forest. Then sending back his servant with his princely ornaments, and his horse, he forthwith began a life of religious poverty. He first subjected himself to the teaching and discipline of Bráhman sages, but he was still unsatisfied; and at last, leaving his teachers, he betook himself to a solitary life of meditation in the jungle. This phase of his life ended at length in the realisation of his possession of great moral truths, and an irresistible impulse to propagate them. In the language of his creed, he knew that he had become a Buddha, to enlighten an ignorant and miserable world, and deliver it from pain and sorrow by the wisdom which he had reached.

His teaching was expressed in five great commandments, against killing, stealing, adultery, lying, and intoxication. This law of right conduct was supported by the doctrine of the transmigration of the soul, according to which every thought, word, and deed, was to be punished or rewarded in a succession of lives of higher or lower condition, according as it conformed to the principles of self-control, kindness to man, and respect for life.

Buddha not only taught these doctrines, but also organised his disciples into a society for the cultivation and diffusion of his rule of life. Missionaries and monks henceforward became among the most characteristic features of Buddhism, and monasteries, memorial pillars, and topes (relic-mounds), arose as the architectural evidence of its diffusion.

**Buddhism in India.** Buddhism had a great influence in India, northern, central, and southern, for some 800 years, but eventually lost its hold on the people of India, and was supplanted by the rising influences of Hinduism, leaving however a permanent impress of mildness and gentleness on Hindu character and habits. During the period of its ascendency in India, Buddhism had gained a hold on Burma, Ceylon, Nepál, and Thibet, and it remains the religion of these countries to the present day.

**Hinduism.** The decline of the influence of Buddhism in India is connected with the rise of Hinduism, which seems to represent a revival of the ancient Vedic religion, largely modified by the religions of the earlier races whom the Aryans absorbed.

In Hinduism,—by which term the religion of the Hindus in its present form is described—theoretically, the Supreme Deity is regarded as worshipped under many manifestations, of which the first and highest are Brahma, Vishnu, and Siva, constituting what is known as the **Trimurti** or Hindu Triad. Practically the various divinities or manifestations of the Divine Power which form the Hindu Pantheon, in the present day range themselves in two groups, one of which has for its centre **Vishnu**, the Preserver, and the other **Siva**, the Destroyer and Reproducer, **Brahma**, the Creator, hardly receiving definite worship.

**Vishnuism** appeals to the affections and **Sivaism** to the fears of the worshippers. The former admits only the offering of fruit and flowers, but the latter, as would be expected, leads to cruel, disgusting, and degrading rites, scarcely repressed by the dread of the strong arm of the British Government. It is found that Vishnuism is the religion of the more intelligent merchant and trading classes, while Sivaism attracts the lower, ruder, and less cultivated classes of Hindus. It must be observed that all forms of Hinduism are regarded as equally orthodox, and there is no antagonism or antipathy beween their adherents. Besides this public religion, however, every village and family has its own peculiar sacred token or emblem, some tree or stone, with special cult, days and acts of worship. This variety is multiplied by continual change. New holy places and persons are continually obtaining popular reverence and worship, so that, when closely observed, Hinduism seems in a continual state of disintegration. All these variations, however, are recognised by the Bráhmans as new manifestations of the divinity, whose great manifestations are Vishnu and Siva; and so unity is preserved, and this religious restlessness becomes regarded as evidence of the vitality of Hinduism.

The great teachers of Hinduism were Sankara Akárya, a Bráhman of the south of India, about the 8th or 9th century A.D., who represents a reaction against Buddhism, and may be regarded as the apostle of Sivaism, and Rámánuja in the 12th century A.D., and his disciple Rámánanda in the 13th century A.D., both Bráhmans, the apostles of Vishnuism, which may be regarded in like manner as a protest against Siva worship and ideas.

The **Parsi religion** is the same as the ancient Persian religion as taught by Zoroaster. Its tenets are contained in the sacred book called the Zend-Avesta, which is written in Zend, or old Persian, a language no longer spoken. It resembles in many points the old Aryan religion of the Vedas, but it does not seem to have affected Hindu religious belief.

The rise and development of the **Síkh religion** was much influenced by the political events of the later Mohammedan period, and is most conveniently explained in connexion with them.

## CHAPTER IV. The Indian Campaign of Alexander the Great.

THE earliest event in the history of India of which there is authentic record is the invasion of the Punjab by Alexander the Great (B.C. 326—5).

In the course of the reduction of the eastern provinces of the Persian empire Alexander found himself on the north-west frontier of India, and impelled by lust of conquest he determined to invade that country, which had been hitherto to Greeks a mythical and fabulous region.

**Campaign in the Punjab.** Alexander entered India by the Khyber Pass, crossed the Indus, and advanced to the Hydaspes (Jhelum). Here he found an Indian army of foot-soldiers, horsemen, chariots, and elephants, under Porus, prepared to dispute his passage. Alexander, however, marched by night higher up the river, crossed without opposition, in the midst of a violent storm, and completely defeated Porus. The bravery of Porus in the battle, and his noble bearing when brought as a prisoner before Alexander, won the admiration of his conqueror, and Porus became eventually Alexander's friend and ally. Alexander still advanced, and at last reached the Sutlej, but he was prevented from attempting further conquests by the murmurs of his Macedonian troops, who desired to return home and enjoy the fruits of their victories. He therefore contented himself with marching through the Punjab, and then down the Indus to the delta. There he divided his army, and having constructed a fleet, sent part to make their way back by sea under his admiral, Nearchus. The rest in two divisions returned by land through Baluchistán and Persia.

**Social condition of the people.** The knowledge of India obtained in this expedition was necessarily slight and superficial, but it agrees with that derived from the study of ancient Sanskrit literature. The country was divided into numerous petty kingdoms, jealous and hostile towards each other. The people were divided, according to the Greek writers, into seven castes, and from their descriptions of the characteristics of these castes, the Bráhmans, Kshatriyas, and Vaisyas, can be distinctly recognised.

**Later Greek kingdoms.** After the death of Alexander and the breaking up of his empire, the eastern provinces fell to Seleucus Nicator, and remained for some time subject to his descendants. But about B.C. 250 the eastern part of this dominion became an independent kingdom, known as the kingdom of Bactria, under Greek rulers, who still, according to the evidence of coins and inscriptions, retained some hold on north-west India.

The effects of the conquests of Alexander in India however gradually quite disappeared, and even the recollection of them died away so completely, that no allusion to them has been found in any part of Hindu literature.

## CHAPTER V.    MOHAMMEDAN CONQUEST OF INDIA.

THE history of India during the period between Alexander's invasion and the Mohammedan conquests is practically unknown.    For some part of this time the influence of Buddhism was predominant in India, but no records of the history of this period exist to explain the circumstances of its predominance or the causes of its decay.

It would seem that the country was divided into a number of petty kingdoms, like the Rájput states which have survived in central India to present times.    According to popular traditions, these were continually involved in wars which from time to time gave one or another the ascendency, but never produced any permanent change in the political constitution of the country.

**Mohammed.  Life, Teaching and Policy.**  Mohammed (Mahomet, Muhammad, the Expected) was of a noble Arab family of Mecca, one of the sacred cities of Arabia.    From his earliest youth he was inclined to religious contemplation.    In course of time he assumed the position of a religious teacher and reformer; and at length, when 40 years old, openly claimed recognition and obedience as a Prophet of God.    Persecuted and endangered by those opposed to his preaching at Mecca, he fled from that city, and found a refuge and acceptance at Medina. From that time his authority grew continually in spite

C.                                                            2

of reverses and misfortunes. A strong feeling of popular enthusiasm began to manifest itself in his favour, which enabled him at length to obtain possession of Mecca. This event was soon followed by a general acceptance of Mohammed and his religion by the Arabs. Mohammed now declared a religious war against the Eastern Roman Empire, and invaded the provinces of Palestine and Syria, but he died in A.D. 632, without having conquered any part of the Byzantine dominions. His immediate successors however, Abubakr, Omar, Othman, Ali, known as the four khálifs, quickly over-ran and subdued Syria, Palestine, Persia, Egypt, and Northern Africa. In less than 40 years Constantinople itself was besieged, though unsuccessfully, by the Arabs, and within a century they had penetrated into Spain on the West and India on the East.

**Mohammedanism.** Mohammedanism teaches the unity of God, and insists on submission to his will. It requires public and private prayer, enjoins abstinence from wine, abhors idolatry, and directs the conversion of the infidel by the sword. Its creed is—'There is one God and Mohammed is his prophet.' Its sacred book is the Koran (Kurán, reading) written by Mohammed, and its sacred buildings are mosques, or houses of prayer, and not temples.

Mohammedans are divided into two principal sects, called **Sunnis** and **Shíahs.** The Sunnis, or orthodox, accept all the four khálifs as the true successors of Mohammed, but the Shíahs regard Ali, the fourth khálif, the nephew of the Prophet, as having inherited the spiritual authority of Mohammed, and reject the other three.

**Mohammedans in Northern India.** The Mohammedan conquests spread from Persia to Afghánistán, and thence to Sind, but no part of India was permanently subjugated by the Mohammedans until the 11th century.

In 1001 Mahmúd, the Mohammedan Sultan of the Afghán kingdom of which Ghazní was the capital, invaded the Punjab, and reduced that part of India completely to subjection. He was a most determined and unsparing enemy of Hinduism, and the destruction of temples and idols seemed to be the very object of his campaigns. The most famous of these exploits was his destruction of the temple and idol of Somnáth. He was popularly supposed to have carried off the gates of the temple to Ghazní, and the recovery of these gates from his tomb, and their restoration to India was mentioned in Lord Ellenborough's proclamation after the Afghán war of 1842.

From the time of Mahmúd's invasion the Mohammedan hold of India was never relaxed. During the next 200 years Afghán Sultans of Ghazní, the successors of Mahmúd, all Mohammedans of the Sunni sect, gradually made permanent conquests of the Punjab, Sind, and Hindustan, but the Mohammedan possessions in India were only regarded, during this period, as provinces of the kingdom of Ghazní. The governors of these provinces however soon began to aim at independence, and at length in the beginning of the 13th century, the empire of the Ghazní Sultans broke up, and the Mohammedan provinces in India became an independent kingdom with Delhi as its capital. A succession of wars, intrigues, revolutions, and changes of dynasty, without interest or importance, followed for the next 300 years, until the period of the establishment of the Moghuls as the rulers of India.

**Mohammedans in Southern India.** In the 14th century Mohammedan rulers, known as the Bahmaní Sultans, belonging to the Shíah sect, established themselves in the Deccan, but from military weakness, or from religious laxity, they were far less unfriendly to Hinduism than the Sunnis of Delhi. After an ascendency of nearly 150 years, their power decayed, and their territory became divided into five petty kingdoms, of which one, Golconda, has gained poetic fame.

## CHAPTER VI. THE MOGHUL EMPERORS.

THE nomad peoples of Central Asia are divided into petty tribes or families which usually recognize only the patriarchal rule of their own chiefs; but from time to time, impelled by unknown causes, portions of these peoples combine together into formidable armies under some chosen leader, and pour down upon the civilised nations of Asia. These hordes have been known by various names, Ottomans, Huns, Turks, Moghuls, but when their languages are examined they all seem to belong to kindred races derived from one common stock.

**Moghul invasions.** India suffered from incursions of the Moghuls. During the 13th and 14th centuries the kings of Delhi were frequently called to oppose Moghul invasions of the Punjab and Hindustan. Sometimes bodies of Moghuls entered their service, but they were a turbulent and dangerous soldiery.

**Timúr.** At the end of the 14th century a horde of Moghuls under Timúr, a leader who had devastated alike the Christian and Mohammedan countries of Western Asia, invaded India from the north-west, and over-ran the Punjab and Hindustan. He sacked Delhi and plundered the country with savage ferocity, but at length he withdrew without any attempt to retain his conquests (A.D. 1399). The Moghuls had not then embraced Mohammedanism.

**Bábar.** Early in the 16th century another Moghul force under Bábar, a chieftain who had suffered vicissitudes of victory and defeat in Khokand, Bokhara, and Afghánistán, invaded India from the same quarter. Bábar entered the Punjab and thence invaded Hindustan. In 1526 he gained a decisive victory over the Mohammedan forces at Pánipat near Delhi, and took possession of Delhi and Agra. He was immediately threatened by a combination of the Rájput princes, but he defeated their forces near Agra, and then effected a permanent conquest of the country.

European writers have given to the Moghul sovereigns the title of Emperor, but the native title is **Padishah** or Lord Paramount.

**Moghul Dynasty, duration and character.** The Moghuls now appear as Mohammedans of the Súfí creed, a development of Shíah tenets under the influence of the old Persian religion, which resembled that of the Vedas. Their religion thus contained an element which belonged to Hinduism, and these two religions, now brought into contact, greatly affected each other, though they did not coalesce. There is however an evidence of the possibility of such a combination in the rise of the Síkhs, whose great teacher, or Guru, was Nának, by birth a Rájput, but by education a Súfí.

The duration of the Moghul dynasty (1526—1857) admits of division into four well-marked periods.

1. The establishment of the Moghuls in India under Bábar and Humáyún (1526—1556).

2. The reigns of the four great Emperors, Akbar—Jahángír—Sháh Jahán—Aurangzeb (1556—1707).

3. Period of decay (1707—1759).

4. Titular Emperors (1759—1857).

The period of the great Moghul emperors is the most interesting of the periods before British rule. It was then, while the Moghul dynasty was in its glory, that European settlements for trading purposes began to be made in India; and the popular conception of India and Indian magnificence is due to the reports of Portuguese, French, and English visitors to the courts of these emperors.

**Akbar. 1556—1605. Accession.** The real founder of the Moghul empire was Akbar the grandson of Bábar. His grandfather had been uniformly successful in India, but his father Humáyún suffered great reverses and was compelled to retire to Persia. In the course of his flight, he took refuge at Amercot, a fortress in the Sind desert. There Akbar was born. After 15 years of exile Humáyún recovered both Delhi and Agra, and soon after died. At the time of his father's death, Akbar, then 13 years of age, was in the Punjab, engaged in establishing his father's authority, with the Moghul forces under the command of Behrám Khán, his father's most trusted general. He returned at once into Hindustan but found that Delhi and Agra were already in the hands of his father's antagonists and that a large force was advancing to attack him. Behrám Khán's generalship however gained him a decisive victory at Pánipat 1556, and established his supremacy. In a short time Akbar was master of an empire extending over the whole of northern India, with the three cities of Lahore, Delhi, and Agra as his capitals. Behrám Khán acted as guardian of the young emperor. At length this control became irksome, and Akbar, having contrived to get out of the power of his guardian by the stratagem of a pretended hunting party, assumed the government. He was then 18 years of age. His boldness enabled him to make good his position. Behrám Khán made an attempt to recover his authority. He failed, but was pardoned by Akbar, who thus gave a signal indication of the clemency which peculiarly distinguished this emperor's reign.

Akbar's next care was to reduce to obedience the vassals of the empire who had taken advantage of the accession of a new ruler to assert their independence. His successes shewed that he possessed military skill of a high order.

**Conciliatory Policy.** As soon as he had thus shewn himself capable as a military chief he turned his attention to the consolidation of his empire. His policy was to win over the Hindu Rájputs of central India to support his government, though such a policy was hardly in accordance with strict Mohammedan ideas. By using his military power and conciliatory measures at the same time, he gained over the Rájput Rájás of Jaipur, and Jodhpur, and destroyed the only one, the Rájá of Udaipur, who refused his terms. He had thus two supports of his power, the Mohammedan party, which included his own Moghuls and the Afgháns of the earlier dynasties, and the Hindu Rájputs. The success of his policy is shewn by the stability secured to his dynasty for 150 years.

**Settlement of the Land Revenue.** Akbar consolidated his government still further by a settlement of the revenue, based on a careful survey of the land, by which the amounts due to Government by the cultivators were definitely settled, a measure which secured him the support of the agricultural classes of all degrees.

**Religious toleration.** In religion Akbar belonged to the Súfí sect of Mohammedanism, but if the account of his religious opinions given by Portuguese missionaries and other European visitors to his court can be trusted, he allowed himself to be influenced by Hindu and even Christian ideas. He seems to have been a man of great intellectual power himself, and to have delighted in the society of learned men of all nations and creeds, and he was no

doubt indebted to them for some of the many reforms that
he introduced in Hindu and Mohammedan customs.

**Events of his reign.** His empire was gradually
extended down the valley of the Ganges to the sea until it
included Behar, Bengal, and Orissa, and he was engaged
in the reduction of the Mohammedan kingdoms of the
Deccan, when he died. The later part of his reign was
disturbed by the rebellious conduct of his sons, but he
retained his power to the end. Akbar died at Agra in
1605, at the age of 63, and his tomb in the neighbourhood
of that city remains as one of the masterpieces of Mohammedan architecture in India.

**Jahángír. 1605—1627.** Jahángír, the only surviving son of Akbar, succeeded him without opposition, but
all succeeding emperors gained or secured the throne by
the murder or life-long imprisonment of their brothers and
relations.

**Court-life.** Jahángír is known to Englishmen from
the reports of those who visited his court in connexion
with the business of the East India Company, whose
first settlement at Surat was within his proper dominions.
The Court-life described by them is exactly similar to
that which is familiar to English readers from Knighton's
*Private life of an Eastern King,* only on a scale of far
greater magnificence and extravagance. In the morning
the emperor shewed himself, and received the **saláms** of
his courtiers. Then followed the public **darbár,** or court,
at which the king heard complaints and transacted business. Afterwards he amused himself with shows, wild-beast
fights, and similar entertainments. All real business was in
the hands of his ministers. The general administration was
controlled by his **wázír** (vizier), who was usually a Mohammedan. The finances were managed by his **díwán,**

who was sometimes a Hindu. When the Court moved
from Agra to Delhi, and thence to Lahore and Kashmír,
at different seasons of the year or for state purposes, the
vast assemblage of attendants, military retainers and servants, formed a moving city. The descriptions of the size
and gorgeousness of the imperial pavilions, the number and
caparisons of the elephants, and the stately order of the
encampment, are almost beyond credence, though given by
those who saw what they described.

**Sháh Jahán. 1627—1658. Military operations.**
The next emperor Sháh Jahán had distinguished himself as a soldier in his father's reign. The reduction of
the five kingdoms of the Deccan which had been begun
in Akbar's reign was now strenuously prosecuted. After
several campaigns, conducted by the emperor in person,
three of them were reduced, but Bijápur and Golconda still
retained their independence. Expeditions also were sent
against Kandahár, but they ended in failure. While these
wars were carried on upon the frontiers the country generally seems to have been contented and prosperous.

**Magnificent buildings.** Sháh Jahán is famous for
the magnificent buildings which he erected at Agra, Delhi,
and Lahore, but especially for the Táj Mahál at Agra,
the tomb of a beloved wife, Mumtáz Mahál, described as
a building of exquisite and unsurpassed loveliness.

**Character of his reign.** In the judgment of a
native historian, no prince ever reigned in India that could
be compared to Sháh Jahán for the order and arrangement
of his territory and finances, and the good administration
of every department of the state. Estimated by European
historians, his reign shews simply the extravagant magnificence in which Asiatic dynasties so often culminate, and
which is followed by rapid deterioration and decay.

**Deposition.** An illness of Sháh Jahán, and a false report of his death, precipitated the contest between his sons for the throne. Dárá, the eldest, was with his father at Agra, acting as vice-regent; the second son, Shujá, was governor of Bengal, and Aurangzeb and his younger brother Murád were in the Deccan. Shujá took the field first, and advanced towards Agra. He was defeated, and retreated with the wreck of his army to Bengal. Aurangzeb and Murád joined their forces, and advanced together. Circumstances gave their movement a religious aspect. The imperial family had been hitherto Súfí or Shíah in creed, but Aurangzeb and Murád were Sunnis. Aurangzeb in particular was regarded as the champion of orthodox Mohammedanism, and was sure of the support of a powerful party throughout the empire. The brothers encountered at Ujjain in central India an imperial force of Mohammedans and Rájputs, but the Mohammedans were unwilling to fight against Aurangzeb, and left the Rájputs unsupported in the battle. Aurangzeb gained a victory and advanced upon Agra. Dárá now marched in person against his brothers, and the armies met on the river Chambal. By superior strategy Aurangzeb gained a decisive victory. Dárá fled to the Punjab, and ultimately was betrayed to Aurangzeb, by whose orders he was put to death. Aurangzeb and Murád then entered Agra, and deposed their father, and assumed the government jointly. It was clear that such a partnership could not last. After a time the brothers left Agra for Delhi. On the way Murád was suddenly seized and imprisoned by his brother, and Aurangzeb was saluted by the army as sole Padishah. Aurangzeb had still to deal with his brother Shujá, who had recovered from his defeat, and was advancing again from Bengal. Again the superior strategy of Aurangzeb shewed itself and enabled him to win the decisive battle of Kajwa, near Cawnpore, one of the bloodiest battles ever fought in India. Shujá fled to Burma, and there perished miserably.

**Aurangzeb. 1658—1707. Intolerant policy.** As soon as Aurangzeb's position was secure, he exerted himself to establish Sunni doctrine and discipline throughout the empire. In pursuance of this policy he re-imposed on the Hindus of Bengal the **jezia**, or poll-tax on infidels, and endeavoured to extend it to the Rájput states. This measure provoked violent resistance, and commenced the alienation of the Rájputs from the imperial government. He also prosecuted the reduction of Bijápur and Golconda, the still independent Shíah kingdoms of the Deccan.

**The Marhattás.** Towards the end of Aurangzeb's reign the Marhattás make their appearance in Indian history. They were Hindu robber-clans, occupying the district of the western Gháts about Bombay, and had been hitherto more or less subject to the sultans of Bijápur. During Aurangzeb's campaigns against Bijápur and Golconda, they became formidable under their leader Sivají, who plundered Surat, and otherwise harassed the imperial possessions, levying **chouth**, a kind of black mail, in a systematic way throughout the Deccan and the southern part of India.

Aurangzeb finally reduced Bijápur and Golconda, and thus extended the imperial rule over the whole Deccan. After the death of Sivají in 1680 he greatly curtailed the power of the Marhattás, but he was unable to crush them, though he was engaged in continual military operations against them during the later years of his life.

The Marhattás gradually developed into a formidable confederacy of states recognising a certain dependence on the paramount authority of the chief styled the Peshwá, who had been once only the hereditary minister of the house of Sivají, but now had usurped its power.    The other states were under chiefs, whose titles were Sindhia, Holkar, the Bhonslá and the Gáekwár.

**The Síkhs.**    About the same time another disturbing power began to be felt, that of the Síkhs.    They were originally simply a religious sect of the Punjab.    Their founder was the **Guru**, or religious teacher, **Nának,** whose teaching might be described as a reformation of Hinduism by Mohammedan ideas.    Their religious doctrines were contained in the **Granth**, a collection of writings in the vernacular by various teachers whom they revered.    They had suffered severely from the persecutions of the imperial governors of Lahore, and, provoked into resistance, had gradually become a military federation.    Their military organisation was ascribed to one of their later religious leaders, Guru Govind.    Every Síkh (disciple) belonged to a military community, called a **misl.**    Each misl was under its own elected **sardár** (chief), and the whole formed the army of the **Khálsá** (the liberated).    Their power made itself felt chiefly in the reign of Aurangzeb's successor, when they began to offer a serious opposition to the exactions of the Court of Delhi.    The severities which they suffered from the Emperor's officers provoked the most intense hatred of the imperial rule, and moved them to continue a desperate, but at length successful, assertion of independence.

**Disintegration of the Empire.**    Aurangzeb died in 1707.    The feebleness of his successors soon disintegrated the empire.    The governors of the provinces made their offices hereditary, though they still remained in nominal dependence on the emperor.    Successful rebels legitimatised their authority by a nominal acknowledgment of the suzerainty of the Padishah.    The lesser governments were in a similar state of dissolution, and every petty

rájá or zamíndár was ready to refuse obedience to his overlord if it could be done with safety.

**Nádir Sháh. Sack of Delhi.** There is only one
event requiring to be noticed before the period of European
influence,—the invasion of India by Nádir Sháh in 1738.
In the course of the frequent wars between the Persians
and Afgháns, an Afghán chief had made himself master
of the Persian capital, Isfahan. After seven years of subjection, the Persians under the leadership of Nádir Sháh,
a robber chief, had recovered their independence, and
rewarded their leader with the throne. Nádir Sháh re-
taliated on his enemies by an invasion of Afghánistán,
and this led on to an invasion of India. He entered the
Punjab, and meeting with no resistance, advanced to
Delhi, which had been the capital of the empire since the
time of Aurangzeb. He engaged and easily defeated the
imperial forces, and having received the submission of the
emperor, Mohammed Sháh, occupied Delhi. The indigna-
tion of the populace, or the turbulence of the soldiery, led to
an outbreak, which was revenged by the sack of the city,
and a terrible massacre of its inhabitants. At length, after
collecting an immense booty in treasure, jewels, and valu-
ables, Nádir Sháh retired to his own dominions.

**Prestige of Delhi.** In spite, however, of this and
subsequent disasters Delhi remained the imperial city, and
the representative of Akbar the legitimate emperor of Hindustan in native opinion down to the Mutiny of 1857.

CHAPTER VII.  THE PORTUGUESE IN INDIA.

**Religious character of Spanish and Portu-
guese enterprise.**  The Mohammedan movement affected Europe and Africa as well as Asia.  Mohammedan
kingdoms occupied Egypt and the Mediterranean shores
of Africa, and the presence of the Turks at Constantinople
and the traces of the Moors in Spain remind us that the
same fate threatened for awhile the countries of Europe.
The struggle against the Mohammedan advance was finally
decided in Western Europe by the overthrow and expulsion of the Moorish dynasty of Granada in 1492, in the
early part of the reign of Ferdinand and Isabella.  It was
natural that the period should retain the impress of this
victory, and that the spirit of religious enthusiasm, which
had been called forth by the struggle, should last after
the triumph of the Christian cause.  The motives which led
to the maritime discoveries at the end of the 15th century,
were religious.  Columbus and Vasco da Gama, as well as
the sovereigns who sent them forth, were actuated with the
spirit of soldiers of the Cross.  Their desire was to carry
Christianity to the new countries which they might discover.

**Portuguese enterprise in the East.**  Vasco da
Gama discovered the passage to India round the Cape of
Good Hope in 1498, and the Portuguese Government forthwith prepared to take advantage of his discovery, but the
object of the expeditions, which they fitted out, was the
conquest of the country and the establishment of a Christian government over it, rather than trade.  For a hundred
years the Portuguese were in undisturbed possession of their
rights of discovery.  During this time they pushed their
discoveries along both coasts of India, they occupied

Ceylon, explored the islands of the Malay Archipelago, and penetrated northwards to Japan and China.

**Old Goa.** On the Malabar coast they established themselves by force of arms at Goa, a city which still retains melancholy evidence of its former importance as the capital of the Portuguese possessions in India. Amidst the ruins of palaces and public buildings, of docks and quays, a few splendid churches, splendid even in their state of dilapidation and decay, still remain to attest the magnificence of old Goa.

**Short period of Portuguese ascendency.** Goa was conveniently situated as a basis for offensive movements either against the Mohammedan kingdoms of the Deccan, or the Hindu kingdoms of Mysore. The conquests of the Portuguese were however confined to the country below the Western Gháts, where they actually formed a Christian state, as evidenced by the predominance of Christianity in that district to the present day, but they never seriously threatened the larger native states.

It should be noticed that the period of Portuguese ascendency in India coincides with the establishment of the Moghul empire, and, under the circumstances of the 16th century, the conquest of India may therefore have been beyond the power of any European state.

Commercial enterprise naturally followed the Portuguese discoveries and conquests, and Lisbon became for the time the emporium of the trade between Europe and the East. This continued until the great political changes of the reign of Philip II. of Spain, when the successful assertion of independence by the Dutch, and the great development of national spirit in England through the events of the reign of Elizabeth, completely destroyed the dominant position of the associated powers of Spain and Portugal.

CHAPTER VIII.  The East India Company—com-
MERCIAL PERIOD.

In England, the development of the national spirit
shewed itself in the voyages of mixed military adventure
and commercial profit made by Drake, Cavendish, and
others of the same stamp.  The information which these
voyagers gained of the resources of those countries, of which
Spain and Portugal had so long enjoyed a monopoly, and
of the navigation of the routes, by which they were reached,
was the immediate cause of the commercial activity of the
following reigns of the Stuart period.  Something must be
allowed for the stimulus supplied by the commercial rivalry
of the Dutch who were endeavouring to take part in the
Indian trade, a rivalry which was the cause of the Dutch
wars of Cromwell and Charles II.

**The East India Company—formation.**  According to the ideas of the times and the necessities of the
situation, the merchants, who desired to open up the
Indian trade, formed themselves into associations, which
received from their respective Governments a formal monopoly of the trade.  This was probably necessary and
equitable, as the **adventurers,** as they were called, had to
take all the risks of defending themselves from the rival
companies of other nations, and from the native powers of
the countries with whom they traded.  An English Company was formed in 1600 and was constituted by charter
a body politic and corporate by the name of ' **The Governor and Company of Merchants of London trading to the East Indies.** '  This was the original from
which grew by successive modifications the great East India
Company.  Similar companies were formed about the same
time by the Dutch and the French.  The effect was soon

seen in the establishment of trading settlements, or factories, as they were called, along the coasts of India and Ceylon, and in the islands of the Malay Archipelago.

**Factories in the Spice Islands.** The first English factories were in Java, Sumatra, and the adjacent islands, generally called the Spice Islands. The Dutch also had their chief factories there. They were keen and violent rivals, and eventually drove out the English, and secured this part of the East Indies as their peculiar dependency.

**Factories on the west coast of India.** In 1612 the first English factory on the Indian mainland was established at Surat with the consent of the emperor Jahángír, who apparently hoped to profit by the antagonism of the English to the Portuguese. It was their only factory on the west coast until the acquisition of Bombay, which was part of the dowry of the Portuguese princess, Catharine of Braganza, on her marriage with Charles II., and was granted to the Company by the Crown in 1668. On this coast their rivals were the Portuguese, whose military and commercial activity however was no longer formidable.

**Factories on the east coast of India.** On the eastern side there was a factory at Húglí in the Ganges delta, near Murshidábád, the native capital of Bengal. Their rivals had factories in the same neighbourhood, the Dutch at Chinsurah and the French at Chandarnagar. There were also factories at Madras (Fort St George) and at Cuddalore (Fort St David). Between these two factories was the French factory of Pondicherri. The positions of all these factories were chosen on account of the facilities which they possessed for loading and unloading vessels.

**Districts commanded by factories.** The relations of these factories to the native states deserve to

C.

be noticed.   Surat might be called the port of western
Hindustan, and Húglí of eastern Hindustan.   Bombay was
near the passes which led to Poona and the Marhattá
country, and to the Deccan.   Madras was the port for the
Karnatic, the broad strip of country below the Eastern
Gháts, and for Mysore behind.   It should be further noticed
that besides these and the smaller stations on the coast
dependent on them, there were agencies further up the
country, as at Patná and Benares.

**The Indian Trade.**   The inland trade was managed
chiefly by a special class of natives (baniás).   These served
as middlemen between the producers and the factors, advanced money to the ryot for seed, or to the weaver for
materials, collected the commodities contracted for, and
conveyed them to the factories.   Part of these native goods
was sent home to the English market, and part was sent
to other places in India, to the Spice Islands, or to China,
and exchanged for silk, tea, pepper and other commodities,
which found a sale in Europe.   The cargoes sent out from
England were usually hardware and bullion.

**Relations with native powers.**   The native powers
were very willing to grant facilities for the establishment
of factories and agencies.   The naval and military forces
which the factories were obliged to maintain for the protection of their trade, defended the coast, while the dues
and payments soon formed a valuable part of the revenue.

**Calcutta.**   At one period the English at Húglí, of
which factory Job Charnock was chief agent, finding their
position intolerable through the exactions and interference
of the Nawáb of Bengal, determined to abandon their
factory and establish themselves on more friendly territory.
They embarked their property, and sailed down the river,
when the Nawáb fearing to lose such a valuable source of

revenue, invited them to return on their own terms.  Accordingly, they chose a new site for their factory, which in course of time developed into the city of Calcutta, 1686.

## CHAPTER IX.  FIRST STRUGGLE BETWEEN THE FRENCH AND THE ENGLISH IN THE KARNATIC.—LABOURDONNAIS AND DUPLEIX.

**Rivalry of the French and the English in India.** At the end of that period of the history of India, when commercial interests exclusively prevailed, we find that the East India Company's factories were already divided for administrative purposes into the three presidencies of Calcutta, Madras, and Bombay.  Each presidency was under a Governor and Council of four members, appointed by the Directors in England.  The settlements usually consisted of a Fort, as it was called, within which were the warehouses of the Company, and the residences of the Europeans.  The Fort was armed with cannon, and garrisoned by a few European soldiers and Portuguese half-castes.  The employment of sepoys (sipahis) or native soldiers, armed and drilled like Europeans, and commanded by European officers, became common as soon as hostilities began between the French and the English.  Outside the Fort was a native quarter or town, often of considerable size, under the protection and government of the Factory.  The French possessions consisted of their factories on the east coast, which were subordinate to Pondicherri, and of the Isle of France (Mauritius) with the Isle of Bourbon in dependence, forming two presidencies, each under the administration of a Governor and Council.  The political and commercial activity of the Portuguese in India was confined to the 16th

century.  Afterwards they played no part in Indian affairs.
The Dutch, after the loss of their maritime supremacy,
contented themselves with the Spice Islands.    Practically
therefore the struggle of European interests in India was
reduced to the rivalry of the French and the English.
The commencement of hostilities between them was one
of the minor operations of the great European war which
began in 1741 and was closed by the Peace of Aix-la-
Chapelle in 1748.

**Labourdonnais.**  The Governor of Mauritius was
Mahé de la Bourdonnais, who had been appointed to the
government when quite a young man in 1736.  He had
shewn a peculiar skill in developing the resources of his
presidency, and particularly in accustoming natives to European habits of labour, and to military discipline.  He drilled
Negroes and Caffres, obtained from Madagascar and the
African coast, and made them a most efficient support of
the few French soldiers under his command.  Aware of the
probability of war between France and England, he made
great preparations for attacking the English factories, and
on the declaration of war sailed to co-operate with the
French at Pondicherri.

**Dupleix.**  The Governor of the French Presidency of
the east coast of India at this time was Joseph Dupleix, a
man who had greatly distinguished himself in the administration of the business of the French East India Company
in Bengal, and, in return, had been recently appointed
Governor at Pondicherri.  He is still more famous as the first
of those 'political officers,' as they are called in Indian
official language, who have studied, and mastered, and employed the politics of the native states for the furtherance of
European interests.

**Madras. attacked and taken.**  Labourdonnais and

his expedition arrived at Pondicherri in July 1746, having dispersed on the way a small naval force which had been sent from England on the declaration of war. After a brief delay he attacked Madras by sea and land, and forced it to capitulate in a few days. Dupleix objected to the terms of the capitulation, and a disagreement began between the two French Governors, which ended at last in Labourdonnais retiring to Mauritius. Soon afterwards this governor returned to France to defend his conduct; there he was thrown into the Bastille, kept prisoner for three years, and released only to die of a broken heart. Dupleix had obtained the assistance of the Nawáb of the Karnatic by promising to place Madras in his hands, but he now sent the English as prisoners to Pondicherri, and secured Madras with a garrison for himself. The Nawáb thereupon attacked Madras with a large force, but was repulsed with great loss by the French garrison.

**Defence of Fort St David.** Dupleix proceeded to attack Cuddalore (Fort St David), the only other English factory of importance on the Coromandel coast. The English made a resolute defence; they took into their pay some native troops, and induced the Nawáb of the Karnatic to bring his forces to their assistance, and they held out until the arrival of an English expedition, which had been sent out on the news of the loss of Madras. The English were now able to take the field, and shut up the French in Pondicherri, but the siege was mismanaged, and at length the English were compelled to abandon it. At this time news arrived of the Peace of Aix-la-Chapelle, by one of the terms of which the French were bound to restore Madras.

When Madras capitulated, some of the English escaped to Fort St David, and took part in its defence. One of these was Robert Clive, the future founder of the British Empire in India.

**Preparations for renewing the struggle.** Such was the first contest of the French and the English in India. It was clear that it would soon be renewed, and as both parties had strong military forces at their disposal, it was natural that they should endeavour to use them in such a way as would strengthen their position for the inevitable conflict.

**State of Southern India.** At this time the state of affairs in Southern India was much changed from that which had existed when the first factories were formed. Then the Companies dealt with Hindu rulers; now, Mohammedan rulers, deputies, in name, of the Emperor of Delhi, were in power. The Nizám of the Deccan ruled paramount in the south, with the Nawábs, or deputies, of Mysore and the Karnatic subordinate to him. The old Hindu kingdoms were represented by petty rájáships and zamíndáries along the coast below the Gháts, subject to the larger states. There was however little real subordination. Each State made itself as independent as the strength of its overlord permitted, and paid as little tribute or revenue as it dared. The relations between the native princes, and the dissensions which distracted the ruling families opened a boundless field for intrigue. There was a continual struggle for power, in the course of which the rival parties frequently made most tempting overtures to the French and the English for their interference.

**The Marhattás.** Before the French and the English began to interfere in native politics the Marhattás were the power to which rivals appealed for protection and support. The Marhattá confederacy was now the strongest and most aggressive power in India. Marhattá chiefs governed territories, which stretched from the west coast to the Ganges, and threatened to overthrow what remained of the Moghul empire. Petty Marhattá chieftains were ready to join anyone who would pay for their services, and Marhattá horse constantly appear as auxiliaries in the petty wars of the south of India at this period.

**French alliances with native powers.** It was evident from the part played in the last contest by the Nawáb of the Karnatic, that it was of the first importance to secure the support of his forces. The present Nawáb, Anwar-ud-din, was for the moment friendly to the English, but Dupleix knew well how to intrigue with native powers, and if he could not gain over the Nawáb to the French interest, he was prepared to effect a revolution in favour of some one more subservient. He easily found members of the ruling families ready to purchase French support on any terms, and he employed the French forces with such effect that in a short time he had established princes in alliance with the French in the Deccan and in the Karnatic. He further secured their fidelity by placing bodies of French troops at their capitals, ostensibly for their protection.

**Counter alliances of the English.** The English were greatly alarmed at the success of Dupleix, and, to oppose the French, adopted the cause of the representative of the rival family in the Karnatic, Mohammed Alí, who was governor of Trichinopoli, about 50 miles from Fort St David.

**War renewed.** A French force in concert with the Nawáb of the Karnatic attacked Trichinopoli, while an English force assisted in the defence.

**Clive.—Defence of Arcot.** As a diversion, Clive with 200 Europeans and 300 sepoys, marched from Madras against Arcot, the Nawáb's capital. He advanced in the midst of a violent storm of thunder and lightning and rain. This recklessness so intimidated the garrison that, though 1100 in number, they abandoned the fort which defended the town. Clive was soon besieged by a large force, but he made a spirited defence for 50 days, when the enemy, after an unsuccessful assault, abandoned the siege in despair. Clive's defence of Arcot excited great admiration, and marked him out for future commands.

**Indecisive operations.** Mohammed Alí at length obtained the assistance of some Mysore troops and Marhattás. In addition a large English force from Madras was sent to Trichinopoli, and offensive operations were undertaken against the French. Their supplies were cut off, their native troops deserted, and at length the French troops were compelled to abandon the siege, and at last to capitulate. Their Nawáb, Chanda Sahib, surrendered to one of the native commanders, and was put to death by him. Mohammed Alí was now practically Nawáb of the Karnatic. Quarrels however arose about the possession of Trichinopoli. The English occupied it with a garrison, but the Mysore commander claimed it, and was supported by the Marhattás. The quarrel ended by the Marhattás joining Dupleix, while the Mysore troops besieged the English garrison in Trichinopoli. Dupleix now made great exertions to carry on the siege of this town, while the English were engaged in supporting and relieving the garrison, but neither side was strong enough to gain any decisive advantage.

**The Home Governments interfere.** The French and the English in India had now been engaged for three years in open war in spite of the peace which had been concluded in Europe. These proceedings had greatly injured the business of both Companies, and the Directors at home had continually urged their respective Governments to interfere. At length in 1754 a joint Commission was appointed to enquire into these proceedings on the spot, the result of which was that Dupleix was removed, and further interference with the native states prohibited. It now appeared, as the result of these hostilities, that the French had established at Haidarábád a Nizám of the Deccan favourable to their interests, but the English had succeeded in establishing their candidate, Mohammed Alí, as Nawáb of the Karnatic. An expedition had been sent out from England to support the commission of enquiry, and with it came out a regiment of the British army for service in India. This was the 39th Regiment, which in remembrance of this honourable selection has for its motto the words ' *Primus in Indis.*'

### CHAPTER X. ACQUISITION OF BENGAL.—CLIVE.— BATTLE OF PLASSEY.

**Conflict with the Nawáb of Bengal.** The scene of interest now changes to Bengal. In 1756 the Nawáb of Bengal died, and, in the weak condition of the imperial authority, he was able to bequeath his government to a grandson Siráj-ud-Daulá (Surajah Dowlah). The new Nawáb was unfriendly to the English, and, alleging some petty grievance advanced with his army on Calcutta. Owing to dangers from Marhattá incursions, as well as to an expectation of the renewal of the war with France, the English had begun to fortify Calcutta, but the fortifications were incomplete and a successful defence seemed hopeless.

**The Black Hole of Calcutta.** It was therefore resolved to retire to the shipping and abandon the place, but in the alarm and confusion the ships dropped down the river and left some members of the English factory behind.

These men, 146 in number, fell into the hands of Siráj-ud-Daulá, and were, by the cruelty of their captors, thrust all together into one small cell, about 20 ft. square, known ever since as '*the Black Hole of Calcutta.*' It was the hottest season of the year in India; their sufferings were terrible, and only 23 survived the night.

**Clive's First Campaign.** When the news of the events in Bengal reached Madras it happened that there was a naval and military force ready for action. Clive, now Lieutenant-Colonel and Deputy-Governor of Fort St David, had just returned from Bombay, where he had been in command of an expedition to destroy Gheria, the fortress-city of Angria, who, like the Algerines of the Mediterranean, had formed a pirate state on the Malabar coast. He was at once placed in command of a strong force, and, supported by a naval force under Admiral Watson, sent to recover Calcutta, and inflict what punishment he could on Siráj-ud-Daulá.

Calcutta was easily recovered, and the expedition then advanced higher up the river and took Húglí by storm. This provoked the Nawáb to advance against Calcutta, but after an indecisive engagement he withdrew to Murshidá-bád. At this juncture news arrived of the declaration of war between France and England. Clive at once determined to destroy the French factories. Amusing the Nawáb with some negotiations, he suddenly attacked Chandarnagar with all his forces, and reduced it before the Nawáb could interfere.

**Battle of Plassey.** Clive had now only the Nawáb to deal with. He, however, was at the head of an army of 50,000 infantry, 18,000 cavalry, and 50 guns, but, as usual with Asiatic armies, the commanders of the different contingents could not be trusted. One of them, Mír Jafar

Khán, a member of the ruling family, partly from fear of
the new Nawáb, partly from ambition, made overtures to
the English. He was attending the Nawáb with a large
force, and agreed to draw off his troops if Clive would
attack. He also made promises of enormous payments to
the Company, the army, the fleet, and the members of the
Council, if he should obtain the Nawábship by their assistance. It was dangerous to trust such promises, but Clive
had probably determined to attack Siráj-ud-Daulá at any
risk, now that he had prevented the possibility of French
assistance. Clive advanced towards Murshidábád, the Nawáb's capital, with a force of 1000 Europeans, including
the 39th Regiment, and 2000 sepoys, and was met by the
Nawáb's army at Plassey. The battle of Plassey was fought
on June 23rd, 1757. It began in the Indian style with a
distant cannonade which did no harm. Clive waited till
midday and then attacked. The Nawáb's huge army made
a poor resistance, and the Nawáb himself soon abandoned
the field and fled.

**Clive makes Mír Jafar Nawáb of Bengal.** Mír
Jafar drew off his troops when he saw the victory won, and
Clive, who probably expected no more, joining his forces,
marched at once to Murshidábád, and installed Mír Jafar
as Nawáb. The native population, being Hindu in religion,
had little sympathy with their Mohammedan masters, and
they had seen many violent changes of governors in recent
times; they therefore acquiesced, without any difficulty, in
the appointment of Mír Jafar. Clive's own remark, when
he entered Murshidábád, and saw its great population, was,
that if the people had been unfriendly they might have
destroyed his force with sticks and stones. The victory of
Plassey is usually taken as the date of the commencement
of the British Empire in India.

CHAPTER XI. SECOND STRUGGLE BETWEEN THE FRENCH
AND THE ENGLISH IN THE KARNATIC—LALLY.

**French Expedition under Lally.** While these
decisive events had been going on in Bengal the French
and the English in the Karnatic had been engaged in a
petty and indecisive warfare. In 1758, however, a strong
expedition of 1200 regular French troops under the Comte
de Lally arrived. It had left France early in the previous
year, but sickness among the troops and various causes had
delayed its arrival.

**Fort St David taken and destroyed.** Lally immediately attacked and captured Cuddalore (Fort St David),
which after Madras was the most important factory on the
Coromandel coast, and dismantled its fortifications. He
proceeded to attack Tanjore in the neighbourhood ; but an
English squadron blockaded the seaport on which Lally
depended for supplies, and he was at length obliged to raise
the siege. The defence of Tanjore gave time for preparations to be made for the defence of Madras, which Lally
presently marched to attack, and after some minor successful operations invested.

**Defence of Madras.** The siege of Madras lasted for
two months. At length a strong expedition sent to its relief
from Bombay arrived, and Lally then abandoned the siege
as hopeless. The English now began to take the offensive.
In the autumn of 1759 Col. Eyre Coote arrived with large
reinforcements. By a prompt attack he reduced the fort of
Wandewash (Vandivásu), a place of importance to the French,
which had resisted an attack made shortly before his arrival.

**Battle of Wandewash.** Lally made a great effort
to recover the fort, but Coote with his whole force advanced
to its relief, and engaged him. The French had 1200

infantry and 150 cavalry, besides sepoys and Marhattás. The English had 1820 infantry and 80 cavalry, with some sepoys and native horse, and Coote secured a strong position, partially protected by the fire of the fort. The battle was fought almost entirely between the French and English troops, the sepoys standing in amazement, to use their own words, at the sight of such a battle as they had never seen before. After very severe fighting the battle ended in the complete defeat of the French.

**Pondicherri. Siege and Capture.** Coote now systematically reduced the various forts held by the French, and at length shut up and besieged Lally in Pondicherri. The siege lasted for six months, and then, as no relief arrived from France, Lally surrendered, Jan. 1761. The fortifications of Pondicherri were immediately destroyed. This was the end of French influence in the Karnatic, and practically in India. Many of the French took service with the native princes, and French corps were a valuable part of their armies in native wars, but they fought as mercenaries, and did not in any way represent national interests.

**Causes of the success of the English.** Besides the military operations there were other causes which determined the contest in India which must not be overlooked. Perhaps the immediate cause was the naval superiority of England, which enabled supplies and reinforcements for the English to be poured into India without stint, and proportionately hindered the sending of such assistance for the French. Behind that is the fact that the English Government was administered and inspired by the genius and large mind of the elder Pitt, while the French efforts were nullified by the abuses of the government of Louis XV. and the feebleness of the administration in the later part of his reign.

**Fate of Lally.** Lally on his return to France was attacked with savage fury for his failure, imprisoned, condemned, and executed with circumstances of gross indignity.

## CHAPTER XII. SETTLEMENT OF BENGAL.

**Clive's jágír.** Nothing could now withstand the English in Bengal. An attempt was made by a combination of Oudh and other states to overthrow Mír Jafar, ostensibly in support of the appointment of the emperor's son as Nawáb of Bengal. Mír Jafar called on the English for support, and Clive with a small force advanced towards Murshidábád, but the dread of the English or some internal dissensions caused the combination to break up before he arrived. Mír Jafar's gratitude was unbounded. Besides valuable concessions to the Company, he presented Clive with the royal revenue of the whole district round Calcutta, known since as **Clive's jágír**, which was afterwards transferred to the Company for an annuity of £30,000 a year.

**Dutch interference foiled.** In this state of affairs a Dutch expedition intended for their factory at Chinsurah arrived in the Húglí river. The Nawáb under English influence forbad it to ascend the river. The Dutch disregarded his order, landed their troops, and moved forward. Clive immediately attacked their troops and ships, and dispersed or captured the whole expedition. The Dutch at Chinsurah, probably afraid of their complete expulsion from the Indian trade, now made overtures, acknowledged themselves in the wrong, and paid a heavy fine.

**Clive's honours.** Clive had acted as Governor of Bengal by the request of the Council of Calcutta, but now that English interests in India were safe he went to England. There his achievements found a just acknowledgment; he was raised to the peerage, and soon after, in 1765, on disquieting news from Bengal, he was sent back to India as Governor of the new province, now called the Bengal Presidency.

**Troubles in Bengal.**  After Clive's departure in 1760 troubles soon arose.  The Nawáb Mír Jafar was utterly incapable of governing, his revenues fell into disorder and he could not meet the stipulated payments to the Company.  At length the Governor and Council of Calcutta removed him and placed his son-in-law Mír Kásim in the Nawábship.

**Shaking the Pagoda tree.**  The new ruler shewed much capacity; he improved the finances, and met his engagements, but he came into conflict with the private interests of the Company's servants.  In the confusion of the late revolutions the factors and clerks of the Company had pushed the privileges and concessions obtained from the Nawábs to great extremes, and claimed for their private trade immunities and exemptions which seriously interfered with the revenues of the Government and led to abuses of every kind.  Junior clerks made fortunes by lending their names to native merchants, who then claimed exemption from tolls and dues.

**War.  Battle of Baxár.**  At length Mír Kásim believing that he should get no redress, and probably fearing to be deposed, began to make military preparations for asserting his independence.  He formed sepoy regiments trained under European officers; he made overtures to the other native powers, and at length, provoked by the English representative at Patná, took the field, and attacked the English with some success; but as soon as troops from Calcutta arrived he was defeated and obliged to take refuge with the Nawáb of Oudh.  The Nawáb espoused Mír

Kásim's cause, and as the Emperor of Delhi was at that time entirely in the Nawáb's power, he was able to secure the presence of the Emperor with his army, and carry on the war ostensibly in the Emperor's name. This policy might have been of service in a war with native powers, but it was fatal in the present contest, for the loss of the battle of Baxár (Buxar) Sept. 1764 placed the Emperor and the Nawáb in the power of the Company, and enabled them to fix the possession of their conquests on a new basis.

**Scandals.** When Mír Kásim fled to Oudh the Governor and Council of Calcutta restored the former Nawáb, Mír Jafar, who paid or promised vast sums for his elevation. Mír Jafar died in a few months, and after some negotiations the Governor and Council appointed as Nawáb Nujím-ud-Daula, a son of Mír Jafar.

**Lord Clive. Governor of Bengal.** The scandal of these proceedings when reported in England caused the appointment of Clive, now Marquis of Plassey, as Governor of Bengal, with instructions to reform the abuses of the private trade and the system of 'presents.' Lord Clive in his letters to the Directors in England describes the anarchy, confusion, and corruption which he found on his arrival in 1765 in the strongest language, and he set himself to work, as he expressed it, 'to cleanse the Augean stable.'

**Political arrangements.** His first business was to settle the arrangements necessitated by the victory of Baxár. To the Emperor was assigned the territory of Allahábád and Kora ; the Nawáb of Oudh was left in possession of his territory in consideration of certain payments, but was to be protected by the presence of a British force, which practically reduced him to dependence on the Company. The Emperor in consideration of certain payments from the

Company recognised their possession of Bengal, Behar and Orissa, thus giving the Company in effect the position which had formerly been held by the Nawábs of Bengal. The Nawáb of Murshidábád retained a shadow of authority.

**Clive's reforms.**    Clive then proceeded with the reform of abuses. He stopped the private trade, and replaced it by a monopoly of salt, tobacco, and betel, managed by the Company, the profits of which were used to increase the salaries of the Company's service. Clive also reformed the military system. He established cantonments, or military stations, for the defence of the country, in place of garrisons in cities ; and he stopped the 'double batta,' or increased pay, which had been granted to the army in war-time, but which had been retained after the conclusion of peace, though this measure was not carried out without much opposition and even a mutinous combination among the officers.

To Clive is due without controversy the establishment of British rule in India; it remained for his successors to develop and consolidate it.

**View of Native India.**    The ease with which the English established themselves in Bengal is partly explained by the state of affairs in Northern India. A most serious blow was given to the authority of the Emperor of Delhi, and to the continuance of the Moghul empire, by the invasion of the Persian Nádir Sháh in 1738. On his death his empire fell to pieces, and the province of Kábul became an independent state under Ahmad Sháh Duráni. This chief found the Punjab distracted by the efforts of the Síkhs to assert their independence, and was induced to attempt the conquest of Hindustan. Four times he invaded the northern provinces (1747—1761); he occupied Delhi in 1756, and defeated the Marhattás, who contested his supremacy, at

C.                                                                 4

the battle of Pánipat, near Delhi, in 1761, but he could not retain a permanent hold of the country.    These invasions, however, caused various bodies of Afgháns to settle in India, amongst others the Rohillás in the immediate neighbourhood of Delhi.    These wars, indecisive in result, weakened all the native powers, and left them unable to resist singly or to combine effectively when the English became aggressive.

## CHAPTER XIII.   WARREN HASTINGS.—WAR WITH HAIDAR ALÍ AND TIPÚ.

AFTER Clive's government nothing of importance occurred until the administration of Warren Hastings, who was appointed Governor of Bengal in 1772, and two years afterwards, in virtue of an Act of Parliament, known as the Regulating Act, due to Lord North, became the first Governor-General of India.

**Warren Hastings, Governor-General.**    Warren Hastings, as Governor-General, was in accordance with that Act assisted and checked by a Council of four Members.    Violent disputes and controversies arose in this Council, which indeed do not seem to have materially affected the policy of Warren Hastings in India, but were the cause of great public attention being drawn in England to his conduct, and to the administration of the Company in India, ending in the famous State trial of Warren Hastings.

**Administration.**    In India itself the administration of Warren Hastings was popular with natives and Europeans.    He had enjoyed a long experience of Indian affairs, and he had taken an interest, then unusual, in Indian literature and usages.    His efforts were directed to establish the finances of the country on a sound basis. In pursuance of this object he placed the collection of the revenue under European officers, but to assist the immediate necessities of the Company he exacted large contributions from the native feudatories, and made political arrangements, which subjected him afterwards to severe charges at his trial. He also introduced the system of requiring native states in dependence on the Company to support a portion of the English force kept up in India.

**Difficulties—European war.** The success of his measures is enhanced when viewed in connexion with contemporary political events. His administration (1772—1785) was simultaneous with the war of American Independence. The encouragement and support given by France to the Americans ended in a declaration of war by France and Spain in 1779, and war with the Dutch followed in 1780. The whole resources of England were required to carry on this war, and it is the glory of Warren Hastings that he preserved the British possession of India during this struggle without burdening the Government at home.

**Difficulties in India.** Warren Hastings had to contend with the difficulties of the disorganised state of the newly-acquired empire. He had also to oppose the hostility of a combination of the three native powers of Southern India, the Marhattá States, the Nizám of the Deccan, and the new Mohammedan power of Haidar Alí (Hyder Ali) in Mysore. Hostilities commenced by an attempt of the Bombay Presidency to reduce the Marhattá state of Guzerat to dependence on Bombay, like that of the Karnatic on Madras. About the same time the Nizám of the Deccan became aggressive towards the Madras Presidency by operations in the Karnatic, but the real and

serious conflict was with Haidar Alí and his son Tipú
(Tippoo).

**Haidar Alí.**  Mysore had for a long time retained a
Hindu government, but recently in the general confusion
Haidar Alí, a Mohammedan, had established himself in
power.  He shewed the characteristic energy of a new
Asiatic dynasty, and was ably supported by his son Tipú
(Tippoo).  He had a French force in his service, and
his army was mainly trained and commanded by Euro-
peans.

**War—Devastation of the Karnatic.**  On the declaration of war by France the French possessions in India
were immediately seized.  Haidar Alí affected to protect
the French, and commenced hostilities.  He invaded the
Karnatic, and devastated it with fire and sword up to the
walls of Madras.  He successfully attacked some small
detachments of the Company's troops, but avoided serious
battles.  By these tactics he reduced the English authority
to the places which their garrisons or their ships could
defend.  His superiority became more decided when, in
1781, a strong French expedition, naval and military,
arrived to cooperate with him.  The state of affairs was so
serious that the Directors broke through their usual rule,
and appointed Lord Macartney, not belonging to their
service, but recognised as '*the fittest man,*' to be Governor
of Madras.  Reinforcements were sent from Bengal, and a
strong force under General Matthews from Bombay invaded
Mysore, and threatened Haidar's base of operations.

**Tipú Sultán.**  At this juncture Haidar Alí died (1782),
and his son Tipú succeeded.  The war continued.  Tipú Sultán
retired from the Karnatic, and by rapid movements sur-
prised General Matthews with part of his forces in Bednore,
and forced him to surrender, and he was besieging the

remainder of the Bombay force in Mangalore on the Malabar coast when the peace of 1784 caused the French to withdraw. Tipú Sultán succeeded in reducing Mangalore and then accepted peace, thus finishing the war with all the appearance of success. The administration of Warren Hastings came to an end soon after the conclusion of this war and he returned to England.

## CHAPTER XIV. TRIAL OF WARREN HASTINGS.

**Popular feeling against Warren Hastings.** When Warren Hastings returned to England his administration as Governor-General became the subject of Parliamentary debates, and in 1786 it was finally determined that he should be prosecuted before the House of Lords by Burke, Fox, Sheridan and others as representatives of the Commons. This attack was partly due to political motives, and was directed against the power of the East India Company, but partly also to a generous sympathy with the natives of India, who were supposed to be victims of misgovernment. The trial opened with a grand speech by Burke, followed by speeches of the other '*managers*,' as they were styled, in support of the several charges.

**Charges against Warren Hastings.** The most serious charges against the administration of Warren Hastings concerned the ways in which he had raised money for the Company, by a war with the Rohillás, by the abrogation of certain payments and assignments guaranteed to the Emperor of Delhi, and by certain acts of oppressive fine and forfeiture. Of the personal charges the most serious was one concerning the death of Nuncomar, a native of Calcutta, who at the time of the contentions in the Council had brought an accusation of corruption against Warren Hastings, and had been immediately afterwards charged by a native with forgery and hanged. The charge concerning the Rohillá war was however rejected by a vote of the House of Commons, and not urged at the trial. With regard to the treatment of Nuncomar, the House of Commons some time before the trial considered the impeachment of Sir Elijah Impey, the Chief Justice of Calcutta, in whose court the trial of Nuncomar took place, but after hearing his defence they decided that there was no ground of impeachment.

**The trial.** The chief charges actually urged against Warren Hastings at the trial concerned corrupt transactions for the pecuniary benefit of himself or his friends. The trial soon lost its interest and dragged on, incredible as it may seem, for seven years, by which time a strong reaction had taken place in favour of Warren Hastings, and he was ultimately acquitted on every charge.

**Change of feeling.** So completely did public opinion alter in his favour and so rapidly grew a better appreciation of his administration that in 1813, when Warren Hastings, then an old man, was summoned to give evidence before the House of Commons with respect to the renewal of the Company's charter, all the members rose at his entrance and remained standing until he had taken his seat,—a most honourable acknowledgment of compunction for the humiliation of his trial.

**Beneficial effect.** The effect of his trial was, however, certainly beneficial. Henceforth Governors of India felt that their administration was watched by the English nation, and would be subjected to the criticism of its representatives in Parliament.

CHAPTER XV.    SETTLEMENTS OF THE LAND REVENUE.

INDIA has always been popularly associated with ideas of wealth and magnificence—'the wealth of Ormus and of Ind.' This idea was fostered by the accounts of early travellers, and by the great fortunes which Englishmen made in India. When, however, the East India Company became by the force of circumstances a sovereign power in India, they found themselves involved in financial difficulties, and unable to make the revenues cover the expense of government. Lord Cornwallis, the next Governor-General after Warren Hastings, and his successor Lord Teignmouth are remembered as the originators of the first scheme which effected permanent financial relief.

**The land revenue.** From time immemorial the ownership of the land in India has been regarded as vested in the sovereign, who granted it to the cultivator for a certain stipulated portion of the produce.

The cultivators, however, did not contract singly for their land, but formed village communities, which, each under a headman and rude administration of its own, held in common the lands of a certain district and apportioned them among the cultivators. In early Hindu times the revenue seems to have been paid by the village direct to the rájá, but in the times of the Moghul empire the revenue was collected through zamíndárs, who were collectors for groups of villages. In course of time the office became hereditary, and the zamíndárs became petty lords who exacted with more or less harshness the highest sums they could from the villages, and suffered like extortion themselves at the hands of their overlords.

It may be noticed here that the emperor could reward distinguished service by a grant of the revenue of a certain district, and such a lordship was known as a jágír.   Hence we find that Clive's jágír, though granted by the Nawáb Mír Jafar, was confirmed by the emperor, Sháh Alam.

**Reforms of Warren Hastings.**  At first the English authorities were content with military possession of the country, and simply required the native ruler to make stipulated payments, but these soon fell into arrears from his inability to enforce the collection, and from the peculation of his officials.   The first reform was effected by Warren Hastings, who appointed English officials to manage the revenues received from the zamíndárs in Bengal.   The disclosures which led to the trial of Warren Hastings determined the Company to take further steps.

**Permanent settlement of Lord Cornwallis on zamíndári system.**  Lord Cornwallis, assisted by Sir John Shore, afterwards Lord Teignmouth, made a settlement of the revenue of Bengal, based on the payments of previous years, which was intended to hold for 10 years, but was made permanent.   By this settlement the zamíndárs became practically landlords of the districts under them, on condition of paying a fixed rent to Government in perpetuity, though certain reservations were made for the protection of the cultivators (ryots).

This settlement represents the **zamíndári** system.   It was intended to extend a permanent zamíndári assessment to Madras and Bombay, but further experience of Indian tenures caused this intention to be abandoned.

**Other revenue settlements.**  There are now two other revenue settlements widely prevailing, the **ryotwári** system of the Madras Presidency, and the **joint-rent,** or **village,** system of the North-west provinces and the Punjab.

**Ryotwári system.**  In the Madras Presidency the Government deals directly with the cultivators (ryots),

who hold their lands at a rent, fixed, after careful survey
and valuation, for 30 years.  Under this settlement the
ryots are practically peasant proprietors, their payments to
Government corresponding to rates and taxes.  In the
Bombay Presidency a modification of the ryotwári system is
found, known as **survey-tenure**, under which each field is
surveyed and assessed for 30 years according to its capabilities.  The ryotwári system and its modifications may be
regarded as temporary expedients, intended to prepare for a
permanent settlement, when experience has determined the
conditions of such a settlement most suitable to the circumstances of Indian cultivators.

**Joint-rent system.**  In the North-west provinces and
in the Punjab, where village communities hold land in common, each village is assessed at a sum fixed for 30 years, and
the village authorities are left to arrange for its collection.

## CHAPTER XVI. Wars with Tipú Sultán.

The administration of Lord Cornwallis was not entirely
peaceful.

**Second war with Tipú Sultán.**  Tipú Sultán was
too much elated by the apparently successful issue of the
late war to remain quiet.  He wantonly attacked a petty
rájá under the protection of the Company, and war necessarily followed.  Military expeditions were despatched from
Madras and Bombay, but the first campaign was indecisive.
The Governor-General, Lord Cornwallis, then took the
command in person, and after carefully reducing the various
hill-forts that might interfere with his operations, he advanced to Seringapatam, the fortress capital of Tipú.  Not
daring to risk a battle Tipú had retired to a very strong
position under the guns of this fortress.  Lord Cornwallis

forced this position by a night attack, in which the whole British force was engaged, Lord Cornwallis himself leading the centre division in person. Tipú's troops were dispersed or driven into the fortress. The siege was immediately commenced, but before an assault was made Tipú yielded. Severe terms were exacted. He was deprived of half his territory, and required to pay a heavy fine.

**Tipú seeks French aid.** Tipú's power was broken but not destroyed. He continued implacably hostile to the British and endeavoured to open communications with the French Republic. At length the menace to British rule in India implied in the French expedition to Egypt under Bonaparte in 1798 determined Marquis Wellesley, the Governor-General who succeeded Lord Teignmouth, to require Tipú to disarm. As he did not comply, war was immediately declared.

**Third war with Tipú. Storming of Seringapatam.** A strong force under General Harris marched straight on Seringapatam, and compelled Tipú to retire into the fortress. The siege was pushed with vigour, and in five days a practicable breach was made. Terms were offered, but Tipú refused them, and preparations were made for an assault at midday, when the garrison would probably be somewhat off their guard. Tipú's troops, however, made a brave defence. Tipú himself took a leading part in the fighting, and was killed in the confusion. When the outer fortifications were in the possession of the assailants, the inner citadel, or palace, surrendered with Tipú's family and all his treasures (1799).

Perhaps no event since the battle of Plassey made more impression in India and in England than the storming of Seringapatam, with the circumstances of the death of Tipú Sultán. The family of Tipú became state prisoners, and a descendant of the old Hindu rájás, dispossessed by Haidar Alí, was placed over a part of Tipú's territory, constituting the present state of Mysore.

## CHAPTER XVII. Marquis Wellesley.—First Marhattá War.

**Retrospect.** The struggle between the French and English Companies had been originally for commercial advantages, but it had rapidly developed into a struggle for the exclusive predominance of French or English influence in India. The wars in Bengal and the Karnatic had decided the contest in favour of the English. The wars with Tipú had crushed the only native state that shewed any sympathy with the French, and thus destroyed the basis for the restoration of their influence. The altered position of the English Company was soon abundantly evident. The extension of the Company's territorial rule which had resulted from the late wars seemed unpremeditated, but it was followed by a period of deliberate and systematic, though not unjustifiable, aggression.

**Marquis Wellesley.—Policy.** The policy of the Marquis Wellesley, steadily pursued during his administration (1798—1805), was to establish British rule in India in the place of the independent native Governments. It is hardly possible to believe that this policy was not suggested by the great events that were taking place in Europe, where French ideas and French arms under the genius of Bonaparte were reducing kingdoms and states to provinces of an empire. His policy was to reduce the various native states into dependence on the Company by concluding with them, as opportunities offered, subsidiary alliances. The general terms of these alliances were, that the native state should subsidize a British military force, to be stationed within its territory, sometimes in addition to, sometimes instead of the forces of the state, and should cede in perpetual sovereignty to the Company sufficient territory to pay the expense of its maintenance, and further should recognise the paramount authority of the Company in all matters of foreign policy. The Company in return guaranteed the position of the ruling family and the protection of the state.

**Subsidiary alliances effected.** The Nawáb of Oudh, endangered by the turbulence of his petty chiefs and by the consequences of financial mismanagement, executed, though with great reluctance, a treaty on these terms in 1801. The Nizám of the Deccan, afraid of the aggressiveness of Tipú and of the Marhattás, and unable to trust his own people, also entered into an alliance on similar but more stringent terms. Somewhat similar motives caused the Marhattá Gáekwár of Guzerat to do so.

**Subsidiary treaty of Bassein.** There remained, however, the four stronger Marhattá states of the Peshwá, Sindhia, Holkar, and the Bhonslá rájá. That of the Peshwá, who still retained a certain suzerainty over the rest, was the weakest. It was at this time almost subordinate to Sindhia, who had recently, since the time of Warren Hastings, extended his sway to the frontiers of Oudh, and held the emperor, Sháh Alam, a state prisoner at Delhi. The Bhonslá rájá of Berar also was in some dependence on him. Sindhia had even at one time seized on the territory of the Holkar family, but recently one of that family had restored the independence of his state, and having gained a victory over Sindhia had marched on Poona to seize the Peshwá. The Peshwá in his alarm fled to Bassein, and threw himself on the protection of the Company, and concluded a subsidiary alliance, known as the treaty of Bassein, 1802.

**Marhattá war.—Wellington and Lake.** So far the policy of the Marquis Wellesley had been perfectly successful, but the treaty of Bassein alarmed and provoked the other Marhattá powers. Sindhia and the Rájá of Berar united their forces and took up a threatening position on the frontiers of the Peshwá, near his capital Poona. Preparations for war had been made in anticipation of this resentment. Sindhia had two armies, one, which he commanded in person, with which were united the forces of the Rájá of Berar, operating against Poona; and a second, disciplined and commanded by French officers, guarding his possessions along the Jumna. An army under General Wellesley (the Duke of Wellington of English history) had to cover Poona and Haidarábád from Sindhia's main army; and another army under General Lake was formed to attack Sindhia's forces in the neighbourhood of Delhi.

**Battle of Láswárí.** General Lake after serious fighting gained possession of Delhi, where the emperor, Sháh Alam, fell into his hands; he then reduced Agra, and ended the campaign with the battle of Láswárí.

**Battles of Assaye and Argaum.** General Welles-ley, in his anxiety to bring the enemy to an engagement, attacked with a portion of his forces the combined Marhattá armies at Assaye. He defeated them, but suffered such loss himself that he could not follow up the victory. The two Marhattá armies, however, separated in consequence of his movement, and he was able to attack the Rájá of Berar at Argaum, and easily defeated him. The break-up of Sindhia's power for the moment was complete. He yielded to the Company all his possessions on both sides of the Jumna, and was glad, for his own protection from Holkar, to solicit a subsidiary alliance.

**War continued by Holkar.** The Marhattá war was

not however ended.    Holkar had left his allies, Sindhia and
the Rájá of Berar, to bear the brunt of the first campaign
unaided, but now began to move.    Ascribing apparently
the defeat of his allies to their imitation of European
methods of warfare, he reverted to the old Marhattá tactics.
He determined to rely on his cavalry, and endeavoured to
inflict blows on the Company's territory by the rapidity of
his movements.    He abandoned his capital Indore, which
was occupied by a British force without resistance, and he
threatened the North-west provinces.    Misleading General
Lake by a movement of his cavalry, he sent off his infantry
to surprise Delhi.    This attempt failed through the brave
resistance of a few sepoys and irregulars, so few in number,
that during the nine days of the siege they were constantly
on duty, day and night.    Holkar's infantry foiled here retired
to the fortress of Deeg in the neighbourhood.    There they
were attacked by a British force, but when they were
unable to hold out longer they evacuated the fortress by
night and retired to the fortress of Bhartpur (Bhurtpore).
This fortress resisted every effort of the British forces, and
held out successfully until the end of the war.    Meanwhile
Holkar and his cavalry were pursued by a British cavalry
force under General Lake, which after marching more than
20 miles a day for several days, at length by a forced march
of 58 miles overtook and dispersed them.

**Recall of Marquis Wellesley.**    Just at this time
the administration of the Marquis Wellesley came to an end.
The Directors of the Company in England, alarmed at the
magnitude of the war and the vast expenditure which it
entailed, recalled the Marquis Wellesley (1805), and sent
out Lord Cornwallis again, with instructions to effect peace
at any price and carry out a policy of non-interference.
Lord Cornwallis immediately resolved to give up all the

territory wrested from Sindhia and Holkar except the district along the Jumna, and renounce all the engagements entered into with the states of Central India ; and though he died within a few months of his arrival in India before anything was done, yet Sir George Barlow, who as Senior Member of the Council acted as Governor-General until a new appointment was made, adhered to this policy, and a general pacification was concluded before the end of the year 1805.

## CHAPTER XVIII.   ADMINISTRATION OF LORD MINTO.

**Conflict between the Directors and the Crown.** The administration of Sir G. Barlow was prolonged through a dispute between the Directors of the Company and the Ministry of the day, which was at length compromised by the appointment of Lord Minto, who had been one of the *managers* in the trial of Warren Hastings, and leader in the impeachment of Sir E. Impey, and at the time was President of the Board of Control, the Parliamentary department created by Pitt's India Bill of 1784 to supervise the government of India by the East India Company.

**Napoleonic war.—Indian expeditions.** In India Lord Minto carried on Lord Cornwallis's policy of non-interference with the native states beyond the Company's frontiers. His administration is marked by the assistance which Indian resources were made to give outside India to the British Government, then engaged single-handed in the desperate struggle with Bonaparte. In 1807, after the battle of Jena, Bonaparte issued a decree interdicting all commercial intercourse with England in the countries subject to him, and by the treaty of Tilsit, concluded in the same year, Russia acceded to this policy, known as *the Continental System*. In retaliation, the British naval supremacy, which was unquestioned since the battle of Trafalgar, was used to destroy the colonial power of France and allied states.    Lord Minto fitted out strong expeditions of Indian troops, which in cooperation with naval forces reduced the French isles of Bourbon and Mauritius and all the Dutch East India islands.    These military measures were supplemented by diplomatic action.

**Indian political missions.**    With the object of counteracting the influence and intrigues, real or imaginary, of the French, **political missions** were sent to the countries on the frontiers of the Company's territory, to Persia, Sind, and PeshÃ¡war.    At PeshÃ¡war negotiations were opened with ShÃ¡h ShujÃ¡, Amir of KÃ¡bul, which afterwards produced most bitter fruits.    These missions effected nothing at the time, but they enabled the Indian Government to obtain accurate information of the resources and condition of these powers in case of hostilities.

**The SÃkhs.**    During Lord Minto's administration the Company's rule first came into contact with the SÃkhs. They were then united into a powerful state under RanjÃt Sinh (Runjit Singh) and were masters of the PunjÃ¡b.

RanjÃt Sinh claimed rights over certain SÃkh settlements between the Sutlej and the Jumna.    Lord Minto refused to admit the claim, and prepared to resist.    However, without actual hostilities RanjÃt Sinh agreed to respect the Sutlej as the Company's frontier (1809).

## CHAPTER XIX.    SECOND MARHATTÃ WAR.

THE Indian Government carried out the policy of non-interference steadily for some 12 years (1805—17).    There was a war with NepÃ¡l (1813—15), but this was provoked by the aggressions of the GÃºrkhas upon the eastern frontier. There was also trouble in Guzerat on the western frontier

with the Amírs of Sind.  But these operations involved no
departure from the general policy.  Soon after the close of
the Gúrkha war, however, there were indications that this
policy could no longer be pursued.

**Subsidiary alliances.  British residents.**  One
part of the policy of the Marquis Wellesley was to station
British officers at the Courts of those native powers which
concluded subsidiary alliances.  These officers, styled
**Residents**, were men of high position in the civil or military
services, and as they had in virtue of the treaty a right
of counsel and remonstrance, they exercised a strong control
over the government of the state to which they were attached.  The Resident had his official **residency**, at the
capital of the state, usually outside the city, but he followed
the Court wherever it went.  The subsidiary force, provided
for the protection of the native Government from its enemies
foreign and domestic, usually consisted of a small British
force and a large force of sepoys under British officers,
forming a complete army division, paid by the Company
out of the appropriated revenue.  It was placed in a
permanent camp, or cantonment, in the neighbourhood
of the residency, and thus served also as a guard of the
Resident, and as a check on any designs which the Court
might seek to effect by its own native troops.

**The Marhattás prepare for war.**  The Residents
kept the Government at Calcutta well informed as to the
sentiments, plans and movements of the native Courts.  In
the Marhattá states there were Residents at Poona, the
Peshwá's capital, at Baroda, the capital of the Gáekwár
of Guzerat, at Nágpur, the capital of the Bhonslá Rájá of
Berar, but none at the courts of Sindhia or Holkar.  The
Indian Government was early informed by the Residents of
the Marhattá states that the Marhattá princes were pre-

paring to combine under the Peshwá, for a renewal of the war.

**The Pindárís.** The Marquis of Hastings (Lord Moira), the Governor-General in succession to Lord Minto, determined to anticipate them.   An opportunity was soon given by the incursions of the Marhattá plundering bands, known as Pindárís.   The claims of the Marhattá princes to tributary payments from the Rájput states, or their own feudatories, produced endless wars, which ruined the cultivators of the soil, and taught men to adopt a life of plunder and violence.   Any leader who could hold out the prospect of plunder easily gathered a formidable body of followers, who were welcomed as auxiliaries in these petty wars, and at other times made plundering incursions into the less protected parts of the Company's territory.   The Indian Government determined to put down the Pindárís, feeling sure that this would give an opportunity of dealing with the Marhattá powers.

**Immense preparations of the Indian Government.**   In 1817 two large armies, of 120,000 men altogether, were assembled, one with the Jumna as its base, formed out of the Oudh subsidiary force and the Bengal garrisons, intended to act on the north-east of the Marhattá territories, and the other, acting on the south-west, formed from the subsidiary forces of Poona, Nágpur, and Haidarábád.   Abandoning the policy of non-intervention the Indian Government allowed and encouraged the Rájput states to place themselves under its protection.

**The Marhattá chiefs declare themselves.** Sindhia was overawed by the large forces on his frontiers, and acceded to the new policy without fighting; but the Peshwá on the withdrawal of a large part of the subsidiary force from Poona to join the army in the field, collected his forces, and suddenly attacked the Residency. The portion of the subsidiary force left in the cantonment made a gallant resistance. Reinforcements were sent to their relief from the army in the field. The British force then became the assailant, and the Peshwá and his forces were driven out of Poona. Nearly the same thing happened and almost at the same time at Nágpur, with similar results. Holkar also took the field to support the Peshwá.

**Second Marhattá war.** The Indian Government had now, as it had expected, another Marhattá war to deal with, instead of the chastisement of the Pindárís, but the vast preparations that had been made brought matters to a quick decision. The Peshwá's force was followed up and attacked whenever an opportunity offered until it was completely dispersed. The most formidable of the Pindárí leaders, Chítú, joined his forces to those of Holkar, and fought the battle of Mehidpur against a British force under Sir J. Hislop, but the Marhattás were defeated. Other portions of the Company's forces attacked the Pindárí bands, which seemed only to escape from one detachment to fall into the hands of another.

**Arrangements after the war.** At length after a short war the Indian Government found itself completely master of the Marhattá states, able to dictate its conditions of subsidiary alliance, and to impose whatever terms seemed necessary for a permanent pacification. The Peshwá and the Rájá of Berar were deposed. The territory of the Peshwá was annexed to the Bombay Presidency, and a large portion of Berar with some other territory was formed into the present Central Provinces. The states of Indore and Berar, both under rájás in their minority, were placed under the administration of Residents, and a complete suppression of the Pindárís was secured by some conciliatory measures.

**Pacification of Southern India.** The arrangements then made have lasted without serious alteration to present times, and have introduced a new period of peaceful industry and progress. Except during the period of the Mutiny of 1857, the history of these provinces since the second Marhattá war is only a record of the efforts of the Indian Government to find the best methods of assessing the revenue on the land, of administering justice without errors and without delay, and of reclaiming the wild tribes of the hills, the Kols, and Bhíls, and Gonds, to civilisation and settled habits of life.

The second Marhattá war (1817—19) definitely settled the position of the Company as the paramount power in India.

CHAPTER XX. INDIAN ADMINISTRATION, 1813—33.

THE series of events which ended with the second Marhattá war had quite changed the old commercial character of the Company. Its business now was to govern an empire. It retained the monopoly of the India and China trade until the revision of its Charter in 1813, but only a part of its capital represented the investment in the commercial transactions. The greater part had been employed in the acquisition and maintenance of its territorial possessions. These changes had been followed by changes in the terms of its Charter, as renewed from time to time.

**Revisions of the Charter of the East India Company.** In 1784 the authority of the Crown over the Company was asserted by the institution of the Board of Control, composed of six members nominated by the Crown, who acting for the Ministry of the day practically directed the policy of the Indian Government. The contention

between the Directors of the Company and the Board of
Control, concerning the appointment of a successor to Lord
Cornwallis, practically decided that the selection of the
Governor-General of India must be made by the Crown.
At the revision of the Charter in 1813 the monopoly of
the India trade was finally given up under the pressure of
the difficulties created for British trade by the *Continental
System*. At the revision in 1833 the monopoly of the China
trade was also abandoned in accordance with the free-trade
ideas of the day, and Europeans were allowed freely to trade
and settle in India, the Company reserving to itself only the
government of its territory.

**Character of the Administrations.**   The administrations of the Governors-General, from the Earl of Minto
to Lord W. Cavendish Bentinck, were honourably distinguished by many and varied efforts to make British government acceptable to the governed.

**Land revenue.**   Great care was taken to free the
collection of the revenue from abuses, and to make it as
consonant as possible with native ideas.   The system of
assessment was gradually modified and elaborated, and
instead of having one uniform system throughout India,
the ryotwári and the village systems were introduced, where
the zamíndári system was unsuitable.

**Direct taxation.**   An attempt was made to raise
revenue by direct taxes, but they were found unsuited to
native habits, and after causing violent riots they were
abandoned.   At Benares on the occasion of the imposition
of a house-tax thousands of people sat **dhurna** (mourn-
ing) as a protest, that is, they suspended all work, abandoned their houses, and sat down outside the city, prepared
to starve themselves to death if the Government would not
repeal the tax.

**Native judges appointed.** The litigiousness of the natives greatly multiplied the number of lawsuits. The English judges were overwhelmed with work, and much delay ensued in the administration of justice. Lord W. Bentinck decided to employ native judges for the smaller suits. This was the first recognition of the fitness of the natives to take part in responsible administration.

**Education.** The first educational measures also belong to this period. The rules of the Company required their servants, civil and military, to study the native languages. This regulation naturally led some of them to take an interest in native literature, and to give encouragement to native study and native education. Fort William College for English officials was founded by Marquis Wellesley, and his example was followed by Lord Amherst and Lord W. Bentinck. Other colleges owed their foundation and endowment to wealthy natives.

**Religion.—Policy of non-interference.** The attitude of the Company towards the religions of India was conciliatory, though it could not be sympathetic. Its policy was to abstain rigorously from all interference with the religious customs of the natives; but humanity revolted against the toleration of cruel and painful rites. After some hesitation the rite of satí (suttee), or the custom of burning widows on their husbands' funeral pyres, was suppressed by Lord W. Bentinck, who however thought it prudent to fortify his action by appealing to the words of the Hindu sacred books. Other practices, such as the voluntary burial or drowning in the Ganges of lepers and others afflicted with incurable disease, were gradually repressed by measures of police.

**First Bishop of Calcutta.** It might almost be said that in the early period the Christian character of the Governors of India was studiously kept in the background, but this negation found no approval in England. A stipulation was inserted in the Charter of 1813, chiefly through the exertions of Wilberforce and his party, which caused the appointment of the first Bishop of Calcutta, Dr Fanshawe Middleton.

**Christian missions in India.** It must be remembered that Christianity had been introduced into India long before the times of the Company. The earliest missions date from the 5th century. The Portuguese missions began in the 16th century, at the time of the Portuguese settlements on the Malabar coast. To this period belongs the preaching of St Francis Xavier, justly regarded as the Apostle of modern native India. Some small Lutheran and other Protestant missions were established in the 18th century in other parts of India, but worked under great difficulties and discouragements due to the regulations of the Company. The English Church had hardly taken any part in Indian missions, and was only represented in India by a few Company's chaplains before this period. The commencement of English missions belongs to the time of Bishop Heber, the second bishop of Calcutta (1823 —26).

**Success of British Administration.** The measures of the Indian Government were not always carried out without difficulty, but the conciliatory behaviour of its officers supported by a firm repression of disorder, enabled them to be carried out eventually. The results were unmistakeable. Agriculture revived, waste lands were brought under cultivation, the half-civilised tribes were brought to submit to orderly government. A complete change seemed to come over the country, all the more striking through the quickness of the transition.

## CHAPTER XXI. First Burmese War.

It was natural that the many admirable results of the measures of British administration should make a great impression on the minds of the English in India, the agents and originators of them. An idea that British rule was to regenerate the East grew up in noble minds, which led them to view with disgust the miserable misgovernment of the native Courts, and made them grasp at the political opportunities which presented themselves for extending British influence, as legitimate means for the promotion of the new crusade.

**Burmese frontier difficulties.** The first opportunity was given on the eastern frontier. The Burmese, originally occupying the upper part of the Irawadi valley, had spread their conquests over the petty kingdom of Pegu in the lower part of the valley, over Arakan on the sea-coast of the Bay of Bengal, and over Assam in the valley of the higher Brahma-putra. They had thus extended their rule to the frontiers of British India. Many fugitives from their conquests had taken refuge in British territory. Quarrels arose about their protection, and at length the Burmese deliberately invaded the frontier provinces, and provoked war (1824). It would have been sufficient to secure the British frontier, but instead preparations were made for conquest.

**First Burmese war.** Assam was easily reduced, and Arakan occupied by expeditions from Bengal. A large expedition was despatched from Madras to operate in the Irawadi valley, and occupied Rangoon with little opposition; but the Burmese abandoned the town, and the expedition was soon reduced to great straits for provisions, while sickness due to the climate attacked the troops and inflicted terrible loss of life. The military operations consisted chiefly of the storming of stockades as the expedition advanced up the river. At length, when the capital, Ava, itself was threatened, the Burmese Government submitted and purchased peace by the surrender of Assam and Arakan (1826).

**British Burma.** These acquisitions were treated after the manner of Indian provinces, and in a few years Arakan became the chief foreign granary of the rice-consuming peoples of India, and Assam the chief district for the cultivation of tea.

**Effect of the Burmese war in India.** The difficulties of the Burmese campaign were grossly exaggerated in India to the depreciation of British power, and seemed to offer an opportunity which the enemies of British rule might use. The ruler of Bhartpur (Bhurtpore), believing from the failure of the last siege that his fortress was impregnable, took the lead in disaffection.

**Siege of Bhurtpore.** A strong force under Lord Combermere was immediately sent to invest the fortress-city. Warned by the last siege, Lord Combermere cut off the supply of water, which would have filled the moat, and trusted to mining instead of bombardment for a breach. These measures were quite successful. The mines soon did their work, a practicable breach was made, and the fortress was taken by storm at the first assault (Jan. 1827). This success effectually restored tranquillity.

CHAPTER XXII. THE KÁBUL DISASTER.

THE first Burmese war (1824—26) is said to have cost India 20,000 men and £14,000,000, but the successes which attended it made the price disregarded, and the ostensible causes of the war, the protection of the eastern frontier, justified it. It was very different with Indian policy on the western frontier.

**Preparations for war with the Síkhs.** There is little doubt that the extension of British rule to its natural frontiers, the mountains of Sind and the Punjab, was a part of the programme of the party which had conducted the first Burmese war; but apart from this, it was clear that the frontier of the Sutlej could not be regarded as permanent, and that sooner or later the Company would be engaged in a war with the Síkhs.

**The Síkhs under Ranjít Sinh.** At this time the Síkh power was in its zenith. Instead of a confederation of more or less independent chiefs, the Síkhs were now consolidated into a powerful kingdom under the rule of Ranjít Sinh (Runjit Singh) the Lion of the Punjab, with Lahore for the capital. His rule extended over the Punjab and Kashmír, and had been confirmed by a prolonged and successful reign of 40 years. The military forces of the Síkhs were formidable from their religious character, and Ranjít Sinh had made them still more formidable by introducing European discipline and tactics. The Síkh artillery was particularly efficient. It fortunately happened that Ranjít Sinh, recognising the power of the Company, and perhaps affected by the lassitude of old age, respected the frontier of the Sutlej established in 1809 and remained on friendly terms with the Company to his death.

**Policy of the Indian Government.** It was in every way the interest of the Company to postpone the contest. It was hardly likely that the death of Ranjít Sinh would not be followed by contests for the succession between members of his family, whereas the power of the Company was steadily consolidating, and the interval might be used to reduce or weaken those states, which might possibly join the Síkhs in the case of a war. It is difficult to believe that this was not the real motive that led to the wars in northern India, which preceded the Síkh wars, though the ostensible reasons were very different. The two possible allies of the Síkhs were the Afgháns and the Baluchís of Sind.

**Sind.** The lower valley and the delta of the Indus had been overrun and conquered about 60 years before this period by Baluchí chiefs, or Amírs, whose clans formed the military force of the country. The Amírs of Sind had come into contact, as enemies, with the Bombay Presidency about the time of the first Marhattá war, but the growth of the Síkh power threatened their independence, and, during Lord Auckland's administration, they had concluded a treaty of protection with the Company, granting in return the free navigation of the Indus. They also allowed a British Resident to be stationed at their chief city, Haidarábád. The Amírs were formidable from the assistance which they could draw from the highland tribes of Baluchistán, and from the position of their chief strongholds, which were in the desert tract on the eastern side of the Indus, where the scarcity of water and forage presented great difficulties to military movements.

**Afghánistán—Sháh Shujá and Dost Mohammed.** The Afgháns occupied the mountainous region on the west of the Punjab. Their chief cities were Kábul,

Ghazní and Kandahár. They were divided into a number of families or clans, of which the two most important were the Barakzei and the Sadduzei families. The mission sent to the Court of Kábul in 1809 by Lord Minto found the Sadduzei family in the ascendant, and the representative of that family, Sháh Shujá, was the recognised ruler of the country. But in a few years a series of revolutions completely altered the political conditions of the country. Sháh Shujá became a refugee under the protection of the Company, and the supreme power passed in 1826 into the hands of Dost Mohammed, the representative of the Barakzei family. Shah Shujá, before throwing himself on the protection of the Company, made several attempts to recover his throne.

**The Koh-i-noor.** After one failure he took refuge with Ranjít Sinh, and became virtually his prisoner. Sháh Shujá had in his possession the famous Koh-i-noor diamond, now one of the British crown jewels, and Ranjít Sinh determined to extort it from him. Failing to obtain it by cajolery or pressure, Ranjít Sinh paid a visit to Sháh Shujá, and at the end of the interview proposed that they should exchange turbans, which is a pledge of eternal friendship among the Síkhs. But amongst the ornaments of Shah Shujá's turban was the Koh-i-noor diamond, and so Ranjít Sinh obtained the jewel.

**Failure of negotiations with Dost Mohammed.** Dost Mohammed was in danger from the power of the Síkhs, and there seemed an opportunity of securing his alliance. Lord Auckland despatched a political mission under Alexander Burnes to Kábul ostensibly to conclude a commercial treaty with Dost Mohammed. He offered to protect Dost Mohammed from attack by Ranjít Sinh in return for his alliance, but the mission failed owing to the appearance of a Russian agent at Kábul.

It was then determined to destroy Dost Mohammed's power, and secure the friendship of the Afgháns by the restoration of Sháh Shujá.

**Russophobia.** The ostensible reason for attacking Dost Mohammed was to anticipate the supposed danger of a Russian invasion of India by securing military possession of the two Afghán passes, the Khyber and the Bolan, by which an army might enter India from the north-west. Some colour was given to this pretext by the siege of Herát, which was regarded as the gate of India, by a Persian army under the direction of Russian officers in 1837. Herát was still held by one of the Sadduzei family. A British officer, Lieutenant Pottinger, who had made his way there as an unavowed agent of the Indian Government, had largely contributed to the successful defence of the city, and the siege had at last been raised in consequence of a British naval demonstration in the Persian Gulf. The siege of Herát and the supposed adherence of Dost Mohammed and his supporters to the Persian interest were stated by Lord Auckland as the reasons for assisting Sháh Shujá to recover his throne. A treaty was forthwith concluded with Ranjít Sinh for the restoration of Sháh Shujá (1838).

**The Kábul expedition.** Two expeditions were prepared, one from Bombay to advance through Sind, and enter Afghánistán by the Bolan pass, and the second in concert with a Síkh force to march from Pesháwar through the Khyber pass. Sir John Keane was the military commander of the Bombay force, but his movements were controlled by two political officers, Macnaghten and Burnes. Sháh Shujá accompanied the Bombay force. The assistance of the local tribes was purchased by a subsidy, and the Bombay force advanced without resistance to Kandahár, which city opened its gates to Sháh Shujá. The difficulties of the campaign from the wild nature of the country now began to cause much anxiety, and the hostility of the Afgháns became every day more decided.

**Taking of Ghazní.** The force however advanced to Ghazní, a fortress-city believed to be impregnable. On the night of their arrival an assault was made. A gate was blown open with powder-bags, while the attention of the defenders was drawn off by a feigned attack in another quarter, and Ghazní was taken with little loss. The fall of this city changed matters for the better, and practically decided the campaign. Dost Mohammed was unable to keep his troops together, and fled to the mountains.

**Occupation of Kábul.—Restoration of Sháh Shujá.** After this the Bombay force occupied Kábul without resistance (Aug. 1839) and placed Sháh Shujá on the throne. They were soon joined by the other division, which had also encountered little resistance. It was however soon evident that Sháh Shujá could not maintain his position without further assistance, and arrangements were therefore made for the military occupation of the country. In the next year, 1840, Dost Mohammed after some fighting surrendered himself and was sent to India. Petty hostilities however still continued, and the occupation of the country was necessarily prolonged.

**Difficulties of the occupation.** The continuance of so large a force in Afghánistán was a great drain on India. At length amongst other measures of relief the subsidies paid to the local chiefs for assistance in keeping open the communications with India were reduced. Their hostility was provoked immediately. Other disaffected tribes used the opportunity, and presently the Company's troops found themselves dealing with a general insurrection.

**Troubles at Kábul.** Troubles began at Kábul with

an attack on the house of Burnes, now Sir Alexander
Burnes, and this officer and all with him were murdered.
These murders were soon followed by attacks on the
cantonment, the commissariat stores were destroyed, and
the troops practically besieged. The troops were under
the command of General Elphinstone, who was in ill-health,
but the supreme control of political business was in the
hands of Sir W. Macnaghten. The military and political
measures taken at this crisis were unfortunate, and a general
despondency destroyed the *morale* of the troops. The
command of the insurgents was taken by Akbar Khán, a
son of Dost Mohammed. At length Sir W. Macnaghten
was treacherously murdered, at an interview with some of
the Kábul chiefs, by Akbar Khán himself.

**The retreat from Kábul.—Annihilation of the
force.** After further ruinous delay spent in negotiating
for a retreat of the force, most humiliating terms were
accepted, and in December, in the midst of the winter, the
retreat commenced. There were about 4000 men with
10,000 camp-followers. On various pretexts General
Elphinstone and other officers together with the officers'
wives were required as hostages, but none of the terms of
the treaty were observed. The force was incessantly
attacked from the moment of leaving Kábul, the camp-
followers died of cold, the baggage was plundered, and the
troops, disheartened and in disorder, were gradually
destroyed, only one man, Dr Brydon, reaching Jalálábád.
Sháh Shujá was murdered in Kábul soon after the destruction
of General Elphinstone's force.

**Other British positions attacked.** This tremendous disaster was followed by attempts to reduce the
British posts throughout the country, which were now
reduced to four—at Kandahár, Kilat-i-Ghilzai, Ghazní and

Jalálábád. The force in Ghazní at length surrendered on terms, but was faithlessly destroyed.

**Sale at Jalálábád.** At Jalálábád General Sale, whose wife was one of the hostages, found the fortifications in a miserable condition, and when he had repaired them, they were badly injured by an earthquake, but he restored them again. He was attacked by Akbar Khán in person, but after enduring a blockade for a time he led out his brigade, attacked Akbar Khán and utterly routed him, capturing his camp and retaking some of the guns surrendered at Kábul. This occurred shortly before the arrival of the force under General Pollock sent to relieve Jalálábád.

**Effect of the disaster in India.** The news of the disaster at Kábul stirred India from end to end. Preparations were at once made to relieve Jalálábád and Kandahár; but the confidence of the native troops had been destroyed, and the first attempts to force the passes were unsuccessful. At this crisis Lord Auckland's term of office came to an end, and Lord Ellenborough arrived to succeed him. The new Governor-General attributed the disaster to the employment of political officers and transferred the chief powers to the military commanders of the forces in the field.

**Relief. — Punishment. — Withdrawal.** General Pollock took the command at Peshávar, and after reorganising and strengthening his force successfully forced the Khyber pass and joined General Sale at Jalálábád. General Nott at Kandahár was also relieved. It was now determined that the forces at Jalálábád and Kandahár should advance simultaneously on Kábul to punish the Afgháns for their treachery. Both forces had some severe fighting, but they met as concerted at Kábul. The hostages had been removed to the mountains on the advance of the British, but were recovered by bribing the chief who had charge of them. The force then prepared to retire from Kábul. As a public mark of retribution the great bázár, or market, built by Aurangzeb, one of the glories of the city, was destroyed.

**The Gates of Somnáth.** Ghazní was destroyed by General Nott in his advance to Kábul, and, in obedience to Lord Ellenborough's orders, the sandal-wood gates of the tomb of Sultan Mahmúd in the neighbourhood of the city were brought away. These gates were said to have been carried off from the temple of Somnáth by Sultan Mahmúd in 1024, and Lord Ellenborough in his proclamation, addressed to the natives of India after the return of the troops, referred to them thus : ' *Our victorious army bears the gates of the temple of Somnauth in triumph from Afghanistan, and the despoiled tomb of Sultan Mahmoud looks upon the ruins of Ghuznee*'—words which were justly regarded in England as grossly offensive in style and idea.

It should be added that Dost Mohammed was released from confinement, and allowed to return to Afghánistán, where he recovered his throne.

CHAPTER XXIII. WARS IN GWALIOR AND SIND.

THE effects of the Kábul disaster soon began to shew themselves. It precipitated war in Sind and with the Síkhs, and even threatened to lead to another Marhattá war.

**War in Gwalior.** The state of Gwalior was in great disorder owing to the weakness of its government. The guardianship of its child-rájá was a source of constant intrigue between the rival parties of the Sindhia family. There was a danger that the control of the troops and the general

C. 6

administration might fall into the hands of the party adverse to British interests. At the present crisis such a danger could not be disregarded. Lord Ellenborough determined to interfere. A force under Sir Hugh Gough prepared to occupy the country, but the Gwalior troops, 18,000 in number, took up a strong position at Mahárájpur to oppose him. They were immediately attacked by Sir Hugh Gough with 14,000 men, and after severe fighting completely defeated (Dec. 29, 1843). Another portion of their troops was defeated on the same day by General Grey at Punniar. These defeats compelled submission. No territory was annexed, but the army was disbanded, and a body of troops under British officers, known as the Gwalior contingent, substituted for it, and the government was subjected to the control of the British Resident.

**War in Sind.—Sir Charles Napier.** In Sind there was more reason for expecting war. When the Afghán expedition was prepared in 1838, it was determined to use the Bombay force for the restraint of the power of the Amírs. They were unprepared for resistance, and submitted, but on the news of the Kábul disaster they began hostile preparations, and presently declared themselves by an attack on the Residency at Haidarábád. The Commander of the troops in Sind was Sir Charles Napier, who had been trained as a soldier under Moore and Wellington, and had also had experience as an administrator in the government of Kephalonia. He first planned an expedition against one of the desert forts, which by his skilful arrangements was quite successful, and shewed the Amírs, that they could not secure themselves in case of defeat by retiring to the desert.

**Battles of Miáni and Haidarábád.** He then advanced to attack their forces assembled at Miáni (Meeanee)

Feb. 16, 1843. They were then fully 22,000 men with 15 guns, and their numbers were daily increasing. Napier had with him 2800 men, including one British (Irish) regiment of 400 men, and 12 guns. The Amírs were posted with a dry river-bed in their front, but their superiority in numbers was neutralized by the arrangement of their troops in dense masses, presenting only a narrow front. Thus, only the front ranks of the Baluchís could act against the British troops, as they crossed the river-bed and rushed up the bank, while the crowded arrangement of the enemy enabled Napier's artillery to make terrible havoc. After three hours' fighting the Baluchís gave way. Their guns, ammunition, and baggage fell into the hands of the British, and the victory was complete. It was followed at once by the fall of Haidarábád.

Numerous bodies of Baluchís had retired in good order after the battle of Miáni, and being joined by fresh forces, an army of 20,000 men soon collected and threatened to attack Napier at Haidarábád. Napier, whose army had been reinforced and now numbered 5000 men, anticipated them, and attacked them in their new position a few miles from that city, and after severe fighting completely defeated them (March 23, 1843).

**Annexation of Sind.** This victory was decisive. It was followed by the rapid subjugation of the country, and Sind was formally annexed to the Company's possessions. The change of government was warmly welcomed by the oppressed cultivators, and the generous administration of Napier commenced the development of the resources of the country, and secured the attachment of the people.

## CHAPTER XXIV. THE SÍKH WARS.

THE war in Sind was quickly followed by war with the Síkhs.

**State of the Punjab.** Ranjít Sinh died in 1839, and the usual series of revolutions and counter-revolutions followed, ending at length in the succession passing to Dhulíp Sinh, the only surviving son of Ranjít Sinh, a boy of 10 years of age. He was in the hands of a party hostile to the British. At the end of 1845 Gholab Sinh, who advocated the maintenance of Ranjít Sinh's policy of alliance with the British, was driven from Lahore, and war became imminent.

**State of the British frontier.** Before this crisis arrived Lord Ellenborough had been recalled, and Sir Henry Hardinge, a soldier who had greatly distinguished himself in the Peninsular war, was appointed Governor-General, apparently in view of the threatening condition of affairs, though with formal instructions to carry out a pacific policy. This may explain the fact, that no preparations were made in anticipation of war, and the British forces seemed studiously withdrawn from the Punjab frontier.

**The Síkhs cross the Sutlej.** Suddenly the Síkh forces, 60,000 strong, began to cross the Sutlej into British territory. No troops were ready to oppose them, but fortunately the Síkhs delayed to advance. A large part of their force was placed to observe Firozpur, where there was only a garrison of 7000 men, and after losing precious time, the rest of their force, 20,000 men with 40 guns, moved forward. In the meantime, by tremendous exertions, a force of 14,000 men had been collected under Sir Hugh Gough, and the Governor-General in person.

**Battle of Múdki.** The armies met at Múdki, Dec.

17, 1845, and after an obstinate resistance, continued until nightfall, the Síkhs were driven from their position with great slaughter and the loss of 17 guns. The Síkhs were defeated but not disorganised.

**Battle of Firozsháh.** They retreated to Firozsháh, where the force watching Firozpur had formed an intrenched camp. The British army soon received reinforcements, and having effected a junction with the garrison of Firozpur, numbered 17,000 men. On Dec. 21, 1845, they advanced to attack the Síkhs in their intrenchments, which were defended by 30,000 men with 100 guns. The attack began as soon as they arrived, in order to prevent the junction of that part of the Síkh force, which was observing Firozpur. After terrible loss the British forced their way into the intrenchments, but the struggle was undecided when night came on. The troops on both sides kept their position throughout the night, ready to renew the fighting at daybreak. In the morning the British troops led by Sir E. Hardinge and Sir H. Gough, after severe fighting, drove the Síkhs out of their camp, capturing guns and stores. This success was hardly achieved, when the rest of the Síkh forces, 30,000 strong, appeared, and joined by the remains of the defeated army, prepared to attack the victors, now utterly worn out with fighting, and without sufficient ammunition for their artillery to continue firing. At this crisis the cavalry and artillery were sent off to the rear, by some mistake in orders. The Síkhs however thought that their line of retreat was threatened by this movement, and began to retire. They were immediately charged by the British infantry. The attack was decisive. The Síkhs were seized with a panic, fled from the field, and recrossed the Sutlej. The British had lost in killed and wounded nearly one-sixth of their number.

**Battle of Aliwál.** Reinforcements from all parts came pouring in, and in January 1846 the British force had increased to 30,000 men. Preparations were now made to drive the Síkhs finally across the Sutlej. A force under Sir H. Smith, sent to destroy the Síkh magazines near Ludhiana on that river, fought the battle of Aliwál (Jan. 28, 1846) in which the Síkhs were utterly routed and driven across the Sutlej with great loss.

**Battle of Sobráon.** Other Síkh forces still held a strong position at Sobráon, where they had formed intrenched camps on opposite sides of the Sutlej, connected by a bridge of boats, as well as by fords. It was determined to attack them at once. Both armies were strong in artillery, and the attack began with a heavy cannonade lasting for three hours; then the assault was made. After desperate fighting the Síkhs gave way. It happened that in the previous night the Sutlej had risen and the fords were impassable. The only retreat was by the bridge of boats, and that was now commanded by the British guns. The loss of the Síkhs was immense. The battle of Sobráon, 'gallantly fought but miserably planned,' was on Feb. 10, 1846. The loss of the British was severe, but they were able to follow up the victory, and, crossing the Sutlej, advanced upon Lahore.

**End of the First Síkh War.** The Síkh Government now gave way, and purchased peace by the cession of all the territory between the Beas and the Sutlej to the British, and of Kashmír to Golab Sinh, who now became a feudatory of the Company.

**Second Síkh War.** There were many signs that this peace would not last long, but before war broke out again Sir Henry (now Lord) Hardinge was succeeded by Lord Dalhousie as Governor-General. The war had begun before

Lord Dalhousie arrived in India. The British Resident at Múltán was treacherously murdered. A British force was sent to restore order, but the movement spread, and in a short time the Síkhs were in arms throughout the Punjab. One British force then besieged Múltán, while another of 20,000 men under Lord Gough prepared to attack the Síkh army in the field.

**Battle of Chiliánwála.** After some indecisive fighting Lord Gough attacked the Síkh army of 40,000 men with 62 guns under Sher Sinh at Chiliánwála, Jan. 13, 1849. The Síkhs were posted on ground broken by clumps of thick jungle, which they filled with marksmen. The attacks by the British left and centre succeeded, but the right failed, and though the Síkhs were finally compelled to retire it was a drawn battle. When the news of this battle reached England, it was determined to send out Sir Charles Napier, who had recently returned from Sind, to take the command.

**Battle of Gujarát.** But before he arrived, Múltán had been taken and Lord Gough had fought another battle, the battle of Gujarát (Feb. 21, 1849), in which the Síkhs were utterly routed with the loss of everything. A small body escaped from the field, but they were followed so vigorously that they were compelled to surrender. This ended the war.

**Annexation of the Punjab.** Lord Dalhousie now declared the kingdom of the Punjab at an end, and annexed the whole Síkh territory to the Company's dominions. The Síkhs accepted the annexation. Prudent measures were taken for the government of the Punjab, and the Síkhs became loyal and faithful to the Company's rule.

## CHAPTER XXV. ADMINISTRATION OF LORD DALHOUSIE.

THE wars in Sind and the Punjab had extended the Company's rule to the great mountain ranges, which must be regarded as the natural frontiers of India in that direction. Subsequent extension has been, as a fact, entirely on the eastern side. Lord Dalhousie, appointed Governor-General in 1848, commenced his administration with the second Síkh war, but during the rest of his long term of government (1848—56) he was able to devote himself without interruption to the work of improving the condition of the people, and developing the resources of the country.

**Administration of Sind and the Punjab.** The revenue settlements of the older parts of the Company's territory had produced good results in the thriving and contented condition of the cultivators. The experience gained in the working of these settlements enabled Lord Dalhousie to introduce into Sind and the Punjab a system of administration, which by providing a sense of security of tenure conciliated the conquered and attached them to British rule. The credit of these measures belongs largely to John Lawrence and his elder brother Henry Lawrence, who ruled the Punjab with absolute but large-minded sway and carried out successfully the ideas of Lord Dalhousie.

**Roads and Railways.** At the same time were planned large and comprehensive schemes of communication between the various parts of India and between India and England. With this object the Grand Trunk Road, running from Calcutta up the Ganges valley to Agra and Delhi, was extended through the Punjab to Lahore and Peshá-war, and other roads were made in various directions across India of scarcely less magnitude. These roads, which were continued by a multitude of district roads, effected an immense improvement in the communication between different parts of the country. The same period also saw the commencement of the great railways which, starting from Calcutta, Madras, and Bombay, have ruthlessly superseded the old modes of travel, by dák-palanquin and elephant, and robbed a journey in India of all its picturesque associations of elephants and camels and bullock-carts, tents, bearers, coolies and syces, servants armed with spears and Sepoy escort (Heber's Journey, 1824—25). These railways have however given large facilities for the extension of trade, and have also greatly assisted in strengthening the military occupation of the country. The means of communication were further developed by telegraph-lines connecting the most important stations.

**Overland Route.** India was also brought into closer communication with England by the development of the Overland Route in 1840. Steam navigation had shortened the voyage round the Cape from the dreary length of four months and a half, which the old East Indiaman considered a fair passage, to a more reasonable period of 75 days. By the Overland Route the traveller to India steamed from Southampton to Gibraltar, and so through the Mediterranean to Alexandria. A short railway journey of 120 miles brought him to Cairo; thence by mule-cart and camel he was carried across the desert to Suez. There embarking in the grand steamers of the Peninsular and Oriental line he reached Bombay in 11 or 12 days, having taken about 30 days for the whole journey. The capabilities of this route have been immensely improved by the construction of the Suez Canal (1869) from Port Said to Suez, through which the Indian steamers pass in 17 hours into the Red Sea, avoiding all the delays and expense of the desert-journey, and making the voyage from London to Bombay in 25 days.

**Irrigation works.**   The improvement of the means of irrigation in those districts of India which have an insufficient or uncertain rainfall was also taken in hand.   New canals in connexion with the Ganges, the Jumna, and the Indus were commenced, or old canals were restored, causing an immense outlay of public money, but promising ample returns in the future by the extension of the cultivated area and the enrichment of the cultivators.

**Annexation of native states.—Oudh.**   Political measures with the same tendency accompanied these measures of internal improvement.   A large part of India was still under native government, though protected and controlled by the Company.   The miserable condition of the subjects of these states was most marked in comparison with the growing prosperity of those under the Company's rule. The misrule of the native Governments, secure under British protection, was no longer checked by the fear of popular outbreaks, and it seemed a measure of justice for the paramount power to interfere.   Moved by these circumstances, and probably encouraged by the success of the annexation of Sind and the Punjab, Lord Dalhousie began to annex the native states, as opportunities offered by the failure of heirs in the ruling families, or by breaches of treaty.   At length in 1856, shortly before the end of his administration, he annexed, on the plea of gross and continued misgovernment, the kingdom of Oudh, which had been under British protection since the times of Warren Hastings and which, though the internal government was disgraceful, had been always faithful as an ally.   This annexation was carried out without resistance at the time, but was intimately connected with the Sepoy Mutiny in the time of the next Governor-General.

CHAPTER XXVI.  THE MUTINY OF 1857.

THE effect of the great measures of Lord Dalhousie was suddenly arrested and the stability of British government in India itself imperilled by the outbreak of a general mutiny in the native army of the Bengal Presidency.

**Causes of the Mutiny.**  The causes are to be found in the hostility of the large class of native landholders affected by the annexation of Oudh.  It happened that the native regiments of the Bengal army were largely recruited from Oudh, and the Sepoys from that province naturally shared the feelings of their countrymen.  The disaffection was increased by an undefined dread of the many changes taking place throughout India, of which the railways and telegraph lines were significant evidences.  There was also one change that particularly affected the Sepoys.  It had been determined to arm the Indian army with the Enfield rifle, a weapon which had been recently, since the Crimean war, substituted for the old musket in the British army.  Detachments from the native regiments were collected for instruction with the new weapon.  The report was spread that the rifle cartridges were greased with the fat of pigs and cows, and that the introduction of the new weapon was part of a plan to turn Hindus and Mohammedans into Christians.  The return of the detachments to their regiments spread the suspicion more widely, and before the military authorities could realise the danger the whole of the Bengal army was ready to mutiny.

**Mutinous state of regiments.**  There had been signs of a mutinous disposition in the Bengal native regiments for some time.  Regiments had mutinied when ordered for service in Afghánistán, Sind, and Burma, but the English officers of native regiments would not distrust their men, each officer believing that his own regiment was loyal, whatever the others might be.  No precautions were therefore taken.

**Outbreak at Meerut.**  The mutiny began at the cantonment of Meerut near Delhi on Sunday evening, May 10th, 1857.  A commotion was heard in the native lines ; the officers went down to see what it meant, but as soon as they appeared, they were shot down by the mutineers.  This was followed by a general attack by the rabble on the houses of English residents, and the savage massacre of all who fell into their hands.  There was a British force in the cantonment sufficiently large to have crushed the mutiny, but they were taken by surprise, and stood on the defensive during the night of the outbreak, and so allowed the mutinous regiments to march off with impunity to Delhi.  This city still retained the prestige of its ancient importance as the capital of the Moghul empire, and the representative of the Moghul emperors, Mohammed Bahádur Sháh, a pensioner of the Company, with the title of King of Delhi, resided in the old imperial palace.

**Mutineers seize Delhi—joined by the king and his sons.**  At Delhi the mutineers were joined by the whole garrison, which consisted of native troops, and by the king of Delhi and his sons.  This gross ingratitude of the imperial family, who owed everything to British protection, gave the character of a national rising to what had been only a Sepoy mutiny.  The mutiny then spread unchecked from station to station in the Ganges valley.

**Incidents at stations.**  Everywhere the same incidents were repeated.  The first warnings were incendiary fires in the cantonments.  These warnings generally failed to shake the confidence of officers in their men, but an outbreak always followed.  The treasury was plundered ;

the gaols were broken open; the Europeans, men, women
and children, who escaped immediate massacre, collecting
in small parties tried to make their way to some native
ruler who remained loyal, and perhaps after terrible perils
they reached at last some of the positions which their
countrymen still managed to hold.

**Distribution of British troops.** It happened that
at the outbreak of the mutiny there were few British regiments in Bengal. An expedition of British and native
regiments had lately been sent to Persia, in consequence
of the occupation of Herát by Persian troops; and the
British regiments in India were chiefly stationed in the
Punjab. The state of affairs at the end of May was truly
most critical. There was even a panic at Calcutta. Fortunately at this crisis the troops that had been engaged in
the Persian expedition were returning to India, and some of
them had reached Bombay. The British regiments were
summoned by telegram to Calcutta, and after disarming
the native regiments in the neighbourhood were sent up
the country by the new railway and the Grand Trunk Road
to Patná, and thence by steamer and by road, party after
party, to the relief of the various stations.

**Arrah.—Defence and relief.** The first success
was the relief of Arrah, where a few Englishmen, engaged
in the construction of the new railway, and a small Síkh
detachment of 50 men, were holding out in a house, which
they had roughly fortified, against the mutineers from Allahábád and Benares and the disaffected natives of the district.

**Delhi—Cawnpore—Lucknow.** The vital contest
was at Delhi, Cawnpore, and Lucknow. At Delhi the
mutineers had a splendid centre for military operations,
plenty of military stores and the sympathy of the populace.

Soon the whole of the Sepoy regiments of the district had collected there.   Fortunately they had no capable leaders, and so they allowed themselves to be besieged by the small force of British troops which had been stationed in the district.   Sir John Lawrence, the Governor of the Punjab, strained every nerve to supply the besiegers with siege guns and stores, and reinforced them with every British soldier in his province and with the flower of the Síkh regiments, who longed to avenge by the sack of Delhi the unforgotten persecution of their religion.

At Cawnpore, Nána Sáhib, the adopted son and heir of the deposed Peshwá, had taken the lead of the mutineers and was closely besieging a handful of English soldiers and civilians with women and children in a hastily constructed, badly planned intrenchment.   At Lucknow more skilful arrangements for defence had been made.   By the forethought of Sir Henry Lawrence, the governor of Oudh, the Residency and neighbouring buildings had been converted into a defensible position and provided with necessary stores.

**Efforts for relief.**   At Calcutta, the Governor-General, Lord Canning, bent all his energies to organise a force for the relief of Cawnpore and Lucknow.

**Massacre of Cawnpore.**   But before it arrived the defenders of Cawnpore had been destroyed.   They had been induced to abandon their intrenchment by a promise of Nána Sáhib to provide boats for their conveyance to Allahábád, but as soon as they were embarked the boats were fired on, the men killed, and the women and children spared only to be butchered at the approach of the relieving force.   The sight of this butchery still fresh when the troops entered Cawnpore maddened the soldiers and provoked a terrible though just retaliation.

**First relief of Lucknow.** From Cawnpore the relieving force under General Havelock and Brigadier Neill, who fell in the fighting, after four ineffectual attempts fought its way into Lucknow, and joined the English in the Residency. Relief was urgently needed. The defenders had held out for 87 days. During that time they had been constantly under fire, constantly engaged in mining and countermining. They had repulsed four general assaults, and their endurance had been taxed to the utmost. Sir Henry Lawrence had been killed by a shell early in the siege, and many others had been lost by wounds or sickness. The arrival of these succours secured the safety of the Residency, but the mutineers still held the city and continued the siege.

**Reception of the news in England.** No words can adequately describe the feelings which the news of the Mutiny excited in England. The sufferings and the dangers of so many English men and women and the hopelessness of timely relief from England drove people at home mad with horror. The suspense was terrible until news was received of the relief of Lucknow in September by Havelock's force.

**The China expedition diverted.** The siege of Lucknow continued, but the crisis was over. Troops began to pour into India. An expedition had been sent to China from England in 1857, and Lord Canning, in the critical state of Indian affairs, took the responsibility of diverting this force to his own aid.

**Second relief of Lucknow.** A strong force of British troops under Sir Colin Campbell, who had distinguished himself in the Crimea, collected at Cawnpore, advanced to Lucknow, and after most severe fighting rescued the defenders of the Residency.

**The taking of Delhi.** At the same time Delhi was recovered. The British force in front of Delhi had held its position for three months with the greatest difficulty under the desperate attacks which regularly marked the arrival of each fresh batch of mutinous regiments; but, having received a siege-train and all the reinforcements possible from the Punjab, was now able to assault the city. The assault was made on September 14. There were two breaches through which two columns forced their way into the city, and a third column entered by the Kashmír gate, which was blown open with powder-bags. The fighting lasted for five days. At length, though not without heavy loss, the assailants made themselves masters of the ramparts, the arsenal and the king's palace. The mutineers then despairing of further resistance evacuated the city, and left it completely in the power of the assailants.

**The end of the Mutiny.** The king of Delhi fled but was pursued and taken prisoner and his sons were killed the next day. The mutineers were pursued by strong moveable columns, which fell upon them at every opportunity until they were completely broken up and destroyed. The final suppression of the mutiny and the restoration of order rapidly followed upon the fall of Delhi; and in November, 1858, it was thought safe to issue a proclamation of pardon and general amnesty, marking the final termination of the war.

**The saving of India.** The glory of having saved India was by one consent given to Sir John Lawrence, and his appointment as Governor-General in 1864 was the just acknowledgment of this feeling. Many other brave men were at the time marked out by popular acclamation as having specially served their country well,—Havelock and Neill at Lucknow, Nicholson, the life of the siege of Delhi,

Boyle and Wake, who held out at Arrah, and Eyre who relieved them, Willoughby, who blew up the great magazine at Delhi when the mutineers first occupied the city, Home and his party, who blew open the Kashmír gate at the storming of Delhi, and many others, of whom some lived to receive the grateful honours of their countrymen, but many more fell in stemming the flood of mutiny and massacre or in restoring the supremacy of British rule.

## CHAPTER XXVII. THE LITTLE WARS OF INDIA.

THE history of India since the Mutiny is largely one of internal administration, but the defence of the frontiers has necessitated, or at least produced, innumerable petty wars. These wars have been due to the inevitable difficulties of intercourse with less civilised peoples on the Indian frontiers, who, misunderstanding the forbearance of civilised states, and ignorant of the resources of British India, have provoked wars which the Indian Government would gladly have avoided. From a military point of view these wars have made India a splendid field of training for the British army, and have also provided an outlet for the martial instincts of the native military classes.

**Raids of Hill-tribes.** The greater number of these wars have arisen from the depredations of hill-tribes, whose raids have become too serious to be dealt with by the local police, and have required stronger measures of repression. In such cases a punitive expedition of British and native troops is sent into the district of the offending tribes in the cool season. This force, after overcoming the natural difficulties of the country, and perhaps encountering some opposition, burns down the chief villages and destroys the strongholds, sometimes securing the submission of the tribes, sometimes simply retiring as soon as sufficient punishment is considered to have been inflicted. Such has been the character of the expeditions against the Jowakís in 1877, the Pathans of the Zhob Valley in 1884, the Black Mountain Expeditions of 1868 and 1888.

**Troubles with frontier States.** Sometimes these little wars have arisen in consequence of the ill-defined relations between the Indian Government and the dependent frontier states. The Bhután Expedition in 1865 was sent to punish the Bhuteas for insults to a British Envoy, demanding redress for raids and kidnapping; and the Sikkim expedition of 1888 to assert the paramount influence of the Indian Government, threatened by claims of Thibetan suzerainty.

**Wars beyond the frontiers.** Sometimes these frontier difficulties have produced more serious wars. The fear of Russian influence in Afghánistán led to an Afghán war in 1878. The second and third Burmese wars in 1852 and 1886 were really due to the difficulty of dealing with an unfriendly state on the frontier, though the immediate cause of these two wars was disregard of commercial stipulations.

**The Afghán war of 1878.** The Afghán war of 1878 deserves more especial notice from its resemblance to the disastrous war of 1842. The success of Russia in the war with Turkey in 1877 so seriously threatened the interests of Europe that a general war seemed imminent. In order to create difficulty for the British Government Russia began to threaten India, and overtures were made to Sher Alí, the Amír of Kábul, which led him to display an unfriendly spirit towards the British. This was considered to justify a war.

**Invasion of Afghánistán.** Strong expeditions entered the country, but about the same time Sher Alí died and his son Yákub Khán, the new Amír, accepted the British terms, and allowed a British Resident to be placed at Kábul.

**Murder of Resident.—War renewed.**  In a very short time the Resident, Sir Louis Cavagnari, and all his escort were murdered in a fanatical outbreak of the populace, without any attempt on the part of the Amír to protect them.  To punish this murder Kábul and Kandahár were occupied by the British forces.  Yákub Khán was deposed and removed to India, and after some difficulty, in order to escape from the danger of a longer occupation of the country, his rival Abdurráhman, though regarded as well-inclined to Russia, was recognised as Amír. But before the troops could withdraw, Ayúb Khán, a son of Sher Alí, the governor of Herát, attacked and defeated a British force near Kandahár, and besieged that city.  In order to raise the siege a strong force from the troops at Kábul under General Roberts marched on Kandahár, thus reversing General Nott's march in 1843, and defeated Ayúb Khán.  This was followed by the complete withdrawal of the British forces from Afghánistán.  The reasons for this war, as well as the incidents and consequences of it, are certainly scarcely less unsatisfactory than those of the war of 1842.

**Later policy.**  The policy now pursued is to assist the *de facto* ruler of Afghánistán, to make the most of his position, trusting that the strong love of independence displayed by the Afgháns will always make their country an efficient barrier of Hindustan.

CHAPTER XXVIII.    SECOND AND THIRD BURMESE
WARS.

THE treaty which had concluded the first Burmese war
in 1826 was fairly observed for some 25 years, when the
cruel and oppressive treatment of British subjects engaged
in trade provoked a second war.

**Second Burmese war.**    In 1852, an expedition was
sent from Madras to operate with a naval force in the
Irawadi valley.    After some resistance Rangoon and
Bassein were captured, and the British forces soon made
themselves masters of the lower part of the valley.    Lord
Dalhousie forthwith annexed the conquered territory to the
Company's possessions and the war ended without any
formal treaty.    The effect of this war was to place the most
valuable part of Burma under British rule, and practically
to reduce the rest of the country to a state of dependence.

**Third Burmese war.**    This might have continued
indefinitely in spite of the unfriendliness of the Burmese
court, but in 1885 the king of Burma, Thebaw, unwisely
attempted to gain a French protectorate for his country,
and at the same time provided a pretext for British inter-
vention by plundering an English trading company and
imprisoning their servants.    It was at once determined to
occupy Upper Burma.    A small force advanced up the
Irawadi, and with very little fighting occupied Ava and
Mandalay, the old and new capitals.    The king was
removed to India, and his country annexed.    More serious
opposition to the British was made by the local chiefs, who
under native rule had been almost independent rulers
in their districts; and their resistance, hardly to be distinguished from the depredations of the robber-bands or

dacoits, the plague of the country at all times, has not yet been completely subdued.

**British Burma.** The only advantage of the acquisition of Upper Burma—besides the natural capabilities of the country—is the connexion which it opens with the frontiers of China, thus affording facilities for a new trade with the more inland provinces of China, though as yet British rule is not sufficiently established to shew very clearly how far these facilities may be developed.

## CHAPTER XXIX. INDIA SINCE THE MUTINY.

**Surrender of East India Company's Charter.** One consequence of the Mutiny was that the East India Company was obliged to surrender its charter at the next revision in 1858, and the government of India was vested in the Queen, who was proclaimed **Empress of India** with much ceremony, Jan. 1, 1877.

**Imperial Government.** Some changes in the administration naturally followed the transfer of government. The powers of the Directors and the Board of Control were transferred to a Minister, styled **the Secretary of State for India,** and a Council of 15 members. The members of this Council are usually men who have held high office in India, and so are peculiarly qualified for their duties.

The Governor-General, now commonly styled **Viceroy,** holds office for a shorter term of four years. There is therefore less opportunity for the development of any special personal policy, such as is associated with the administrations of Wellesley and Dalhousie.

The Governor-General is assisted by a Council of five members, who are practically Ministers for different departments of the Indian Government.   There is also a Legislative Council, consisting of the Governor-General's Council and certain other nominated members, amongst whom are always some native princes.

**Indian Civil Service.**   The Indian Civil Service is no longer supplied through the nomination of a close Company, but is filled by the test of competitive examination. This has largely increased the field of selection, and at the same time has caused a much wider interest to be taken in Indian affairs.

**Territorial divisions.**   For administrative purposes that part of India which is under the direct government of the Viceroy is now divided into eight provinces, 1 **Bengal, 2 Madras, 3 Bombay, 4 North-West Provinces and Oudh,** with Allahábád for capital, 5 **Punjab,** with Lahore for its capital, 6 **Central Provinces,** with Nágpur for capital, 7 **Assam,** 8 **Burma.**   The cities of Delhi, Lucknow, and Cawnpore have forfeited their ancient honours for the part which they played in the Mutiny.

The native States in dependence on the Indian Government are of three kinds.   The **Rájput States** of the centre retain the ancient clan institutions of primitive India, the government being vested in a chief who is at the same time head of the clan.   The **Marhattá States** are now the States of Gwalior, Indore and Baroda, which were formed by the conquest of various parts of Central India by Marhattá chieftains between the death of Aurangzeb and the First Marhattá war; and the Marhattá princes rule simply by the right of conquest, recognised by the Indian Government. Besides these there is the great **Mohammedan State** of the Deccan, governed by the Nizám, the only representative of the old Moghul governments since the annexation of Oudh. **Mysore** ranked as a Mohammedan state under Haidar

Alí and Típú, but on the destruction of Típú's power it was reconstituted as a Hindu rájáship of a special type. There are also certain small Hindu rájáships below the Gháts, owing their preservation to alliances concluded with the Company in the time of the early struggles with the French. **Kashmír** was a conquest of the Síkhs, and the right of the present ruling family is similar to that of the Marhattá princes. Recently the Maharájá of Kashmír has been deposed for disloyal conduct, and the government of this state is now administered by a native Council subject to the control of the British Resident.

**Imperial policy.** The Mutiny made a deep impression in England. It was felt to be a condemnation of the treatment of India hitherto pursued, and the assumption of the government of India by the Crown was meant to shew that the English nation recognised and accepted responsibilities towards India beyond those which the Company had ever recognised. This feeling has determined the general character of Indian legislation and administration during the last 30 years.

**Education.—Its effects.** The educational system of India has received a vast extension since the Mutiny by the provision of schools of various grades and colleges throughout the country. The education received in the higher schools and colleges has naturally tended to destroy respect for the coarser forms of the Hindu religion. Some of the educated Hindus, forming a recognised religious body known as the Brahmo Samáj, have in consequence attempted to graft Christian morality on Hinduism, just as the Neo-Platonists of Alexandria tried to infuse Christian morality into Greek and Latin mythology. Others lose their old belief without gaining anything in its place.

It is difficult to say whether it is due to the spread of

education or to the influence of Christian opinion, that various questions deeply affecting Hindu life, such as the abolition of child-marriage, the re-marriage of widows, and the education of women, have of late years been considered in India in a way that promises in time changes of the utmost importance.

**Conciliation of natives.** The Mutiny greatly widened the separation between Englishmen and natives. It is pleasant, therefore, to notice that the conciliation of native India is the avowed object of the policy which characterises the period of Indian history since the administration of Lord Mayo in 1869. This policy seeks to associate the natives of India with Europeans in the government of the country. In accordance with this policy some seats in the Legislative Council are now filled by native princes, Hindu and Mohammedan; and natives of suitable education are admitted to the Civil Service.

**Effects of these measures.** These changes have, as was intended and expected, produced a certain approach to European ways of political and social action. Native newspapers discuss questions of political or social interest from the native point of view. Municipalities with governing bodies of European and native representatives are evidences of the beginning of local government. Native gentlemen take part in the management of hospitals and colleges. And recently a native Congress has assembled and considered questions affecting native interests in a way to command the attention and sympathy of Englishmen.

**Famines.—Orissa, 1866, and Southern India, 1876.** In deference to English opinion at home, the Government of India has recognised as part of its duties the protection of its subjects in the event of those famines which, from the irregularity or the insufficiency of rainfall, occur from time to time on a gigantic scale in India.

In the Orissa famine of 1866 it was considered that one-fourth of the population of the province perished. This terrible calamity strongly excited the sympathy of English people, but the results shewed that the relief of such distress could not be properly met by private benevolence alone. It was therefore recognised that the Indian Government must undertake provision for the relief of districts threatened with famine; and one of the most honourable records of British rule in India is the story of the exertions, public and private, made to grapple with the great famine of Southern India (1876-8). The rainfall then failed in two successive years, and for 18 months all the energies of Government were strained to save fifteen millions of people from sheer starvation. As such famines are periodical in India, the Indian Government has directed its attention of late years to provide for their permanent alleviation by the extension of irrigation canals and the improvement of the means of communication, and by other precautionary measures, intended to make the various districts less dependent on local rainfall and local supplies.

**Future relations.** The peculiar circumstances of India made the establishment and extension of British rule welcome as a relief from a state of violence, disorder, and oppression; but the teaching of all history is that such conditions can only be temporary. Some better bond must be found to unite governors and governed. The material benefits of Imperial government, the growth of commercial interests, the influence of Western thought, and the gradual spread of Christian teaching tend to bring various parts of the peoples of India more and more into contentment and sympathy with British rule. The future relations of India to the British Empire will be determined by the extent to which these tendencies can be developed. There is therefore good ground for hopefulness in regard to the future in the knowledge of the large-minded and generous spirit, not unworthy of the great issues involved, in which the Government of India is being administered.

## CHAPTER XXX. INDIAN LITERATURE.

SANSKRIT, the language of the Vedas, became the literary language of India, in the same way as Latin, the language of the Church, became the literary language of Europe. Sanskrit literature includes works on philology and science, but in its general character it is **the sacred literature of India.**

**Sanskrit literature.** Great attention has been given in recent times to the study of ancient Sanskrit literature, but its chief interest lies in its historical value in regard to the origin and development of Hindu institutions and usages.

After the Vedas, from which the primitive state of the Aryans is inferred, the works of greatest interest are the Laws of Manu and the Puranas.

The work known as **the Laws of Manu** belongs to the class of sacred Law-books. It treats of the social condition of the Hindus in very early times, the relations of the four castes, and the duties of government. The **Puranas** are sacred poems containing the popular mythology of modern Hinduism.

Buddhism has to be studied in the sacred books of the Buddhists of Ceylon and China. Those of Ceylon are written in Páli, which is the literary language of Ceylon and Burma, and corresponds to Sanskrit in India. Those

of China are translations made from Sanskrit originals, some
of which are extant, some lost, into Chinese.

**Persian literature.** The historians of India belong
to the Mohammedan period. The dialect of India due to
Mohammedan influences is **Hindustáni,** but the language
of the Mohammedan historians is **Persian. Ferishta,**
who resided at the Court of Bijápur, one of the Deccan
kingdoms, about the end of Akbar's reign, is the chief
authority for the earlier history of Mohammedan India.
**Abul Fazl,** the minister and intimate friend of the emperor
Akbar, wrote the history of his reign and administration.
Except a history of Kashmír, there are no Hindu histories.

**European writings.** There are some accounts of
India written by Europeans who visited the imperial court
in the course of the 17th century, as those of **Sir Thomas
Roe,** ambassador from James 1st to the emperor Jahángír,
of **Tavernier,** a French jeweller, who travelled on business
through India (1638—68), and of **Bernier,** a French
physician, attached to the Court of Delhi about the same
period. But the most important and trustworthy sources of
information are the records of the East India Company,
the reports of their governors and officers, which give full
information about the growth of their power, their civil
administration and general policy.

In recent times the Indian Government has caused most
careful surveys of the country to be made for the assessment
of the land revenue. The knowledge thus obtained of the
resources of the country and of the condition of the people
has been digested in elaborate reports, which besides supplying information necessary for administrative purposes
provide a most valuable record of the present state of India.

## Moghul Emperors of India, 1526—1857.

### 1.   Rise of the Empire.

1526.  Bábar.
1530.  Humáyún.

### 2.   The Great Emperors.

1556.  Akbar.
1605.  Jahángír.
1627.  Sháh Jahán.
1658.  Aurangzeb.

### 3.   Decline of the Empire.

1707.  Bahádur Sháh.
1712.  Jahándar Sháh.
1713.  Farokhsír.
1719.  Mohammed Sháh.
1748.  Ahmad Sháh.
1754.  Alamgír.

### 4.   Titular Emperors.

1759.  Sháh Alam.
1806.  Akbar.
1837.  Mohammed Bahádur Sháh,
           deposed after the Mutiny of 1857.

# Governors of British India, 1758—1888.

## Governors.

1758. Lord Clive.
1767. Henry Verelst.
1769. John Cartier.
1772. Warren Hastings.

## Governors-General.

1774. Warren Hastings.
1786. Marquis of Cornwallis.
1793. Lord Teignmouth.
1798. Marquis Wellesley.
1805. Marquis of Cornwallis.
1806. Earl of Minto.
1813. Marquis of Hastings.
1823. Lord Amherst.
1828. Lord W. Cavendish Bentinck.
1836. Lord Auckland.
1842. Lord Ellenborough.
1844. Lord Hardinge.
1848. Marquis of Dalhousie.
1856. Lord Canning.

## Viceroys.

1858. Earl Canning.
1862. Earl of Elgin.
1864. Sir John Lawrence.
1869. Earl of Mayo.
1872. Earl of Northbrook.
1876. Earl of Lytton.
1880. Marquis of Ripon.
1884. Lord Dufferin.
1888. Lord Lansdowne.

# INDEX.

Printed in the United States
By Bookmasters